The Map of London

From 1746 to the Present Day

Andrew Davies

B. T. Batsford Ltd., London

ISBN 0 7134 5404 0 (cased)

Typeset by Tek Art Ltd, Kent
and printed in Great Britain by
Butler & Tanner Ltd
Frome, Somerset
for the publishers
B. T. Batsford Ltd
4 Fitzhardinge Street
London
W1H 0AH

'That Westminster is in a fair way to shake hands with Chelsea, as St Gyles is with Marybone; and Great Russel Street by Montague House, with Tottenham-Court; all this is very evident, and yet all these put together, are still to be called London. Whither will this monstrous city then extend? and where must a circumvallation or communication line of it be placed?'

Daniel Defoe *A Tour Through The Whole Island Of Great Britain*
(1724-1726)

Contents

Acknowledgements

Many thanks to all the members of my London history classes at Friday Hill House in Chingford and the Old House, Brentwood who have uncomplainingly followed me around the streets of London several times each week, interested in Rotherhithe and Shadwell as well as in Mayfair and St. James's.

Thanks also to Chris Smith for his advice; to David Taylor of A-Z in London; to Fran Hazelton who went through several of the City sections with me; to my agent Sara Drake for her support and encouragement; and to Neelam Sharma of Batsford for being both patient and interested. Finally, many thanks to my family for just being there, and to Jean who has, as always, been my companion and additional pair of eyes on so many London walks.

The A-Z maps in this book are reproduced by permission of Geographers' A-Z Map Co. Ltd, Crown copyright reserved. Ordnance Survey material was used in the revision of these maps, Crown copyright reserved.

All the photographs in this book have been reproduced by kind permission of BBC Hulton Picture Library.

Introduction

Several years ago I came across a second-hand copy of W. Crawford Snowden's *London 200 Years Ago*, published in the late 1940s. Snowden's book reproduced, in 24 sheets, a mid-eighteenth-century map of London by the surveyor and printseller John Rocque. This map had first been issued in 1746.

I began to show the book to my London history classes and it invariably aroused great interest, the detail of Rocque's work prompting people to pore over the streets, roads and squares of Georgian London and try to relate them to the city of today. Then it struck me that it would be a good idea to reproduce Rocque's survey again in its 24 sections but on the facing page to publish a map of that area as it is today. A commentary would be provided over the page for anyone who wanted it. 1987 is a particularly appropriate year to publish Rocque's work: it was exactly 250 years ago that he began his survey.

This nine-year task of Rocque's coincided with many other important events taking place around about him: in 1737 the unknown Samuel Johnson and David Garrick travelled to London; Henry Fielding was about to turn from the stage towards the Bar and the novel; Sir Robert Walpole was at 10 Downing Street; Handel was composing his *Messiah*; Samuel Richardson was writing *Pamela*; in May 1738 John Wesley experienced his 'conversion'. I have tried to convey some of the excitement of this 'Golden Age' – and the pleasure which I have received from working on this book. Memoirs, diaries and novels have been drawn upon, and I have used the observations of individuals both before and after Rocque's day only if their remarks are pertinent to the London of the 1730s and 1740s, namely Pepys, Evelyn and Boswell. I am working on a companion volume to *The Map of London*, entitled *Hogarth's London*, which will concentrate on the visual dimension of Georgian London.

The first section of this book outlines the life of John Rocque and places him in the context of London mapmaking. The second section describes London in the middle of the eighteenth century, sketching out changes and contrasts with the metropolis of today. The third section contains the 48 maps and accompanying commentary. After each section there is a note on sources and a guide to further reading – the place of publication is always London unless otherwise stated. Photographs illustrate various events or people mentioned in the text and there is also a chronology.

Chronology

1677 – The marriage of Sir Thomas Grosvenor with Mary Davies marks the beginning of the Grosvenor estate.

1685 – The Revocation of the Edict of Nantes: thousands of French Huguenots flee to London.

1689 – First admissions to Chelsea Hospital.

1694 – Incorporation of the Bank of England.

1697 – Ending of sanctuaries such as Alsatia near Fleet Street and the Clink.

1703 – Publication of Ned Ward's *The London Spy* in book form.

1703 – Death of Samuel Pepys.

1706 – Death of John Evelyn.

1710 – Completion of Wren's St. Paul's.

1711 – The 50 New Churches Act.

1720 – The collapse of the South Sea Bubble halts development in and around London.

1722 – Publication of Daniel Defoe's *Moll Flanders*.

1724 – Completion of St. George's, Hanover Square.

1727 – Death of George I and accession of George II who reigned until 1760.

1728 – John Gay's *The Beggar's Opera* first performed.

1731 – Death of Daniel Defoe.

1732 – Opening of Covent Garden Theatre.

1733 – William and Jane Hogarth move to no.30, Leicester Fields.

1733 – The Serpentine in Hyde Park is laid out by Queen Caroline.

1735 – Sir Robert Walpole moves into 10 Downing Street as 1st Lord of the Treasury or Prime Minister; resigns in 1742.

1736 – Death of Sir Nicholas Hawksmoor.

1737 – Samuel Johnson and David Garrick arrive in London.

1737 – John Rocque begins his survey of London.

1739 – The Foundling Hospital initiated by Thomas Coram receives its royal charter.

1739 – John Wesley converts a foundry into his first Methodist Meeting Hall.

1739-40 – A Frost Fair held on the Thames.

1741 – First performance of Handel's *Messiah*.

1741 – David Garrick first makes his name in Shakespeare's *Richard III*.

1742 – The Ranelagh Gardens in Chelsea are opened.

1746 – Rocque's map of London published.

1747 – Last execution at Tower Hill; the scaffold is removed.

1748 – Appointment of Henry Fielding as magistrate for Westminster; the next year sees the publication of his *Tom Jones* and the founding of the Bow Street Runners.

1750 – Westminster Bridge, the second over the Thames, is opened.

1751 – Hogarth's engraving *Gin Lane*; the Licensing Act regulates the distilling and sale of gin.

1757 – Opening of the New Road – our Marylebone and Euston Roads.

1759 – The British Museum is first opened to the public.

1760 – Three of the City gates are pulled down; the other four soon follow.

1761 – Passage of the Westminster Paving and Lighting Act.

1762 – Ending of Southwark Fair.

1762-63 – The young James Boswell stays in London and keeps his *London Journal*.

1766 – The Fleet river is completely covered over.

1783 – The last execution held at Tyburn, the first at Newgate.

1802 – West India Dock opened.

1807 – Gas first used in London.

1813 – Work starts on John Nash's Regent Street.

1820s – Buckingham House is turned into Buckingham Palace.

1827 – The Turnpike Act: several are removed.

1829 – Founding of the Metropolitan Police by Sir Robert Peel.

1831 – Opening of the new London Bridge.

1836 – Building of London Bridge station, the first in London.

1843 – Opening of the Brunels' Thames Tunnel between Wapping and Rotherhithe.

1851 – Opening of Victoria Street in Westminster – example of Victorian roadbuilding programme.

1863 – The first section of the Underground opened between Farringdon Street and Paddington.

John Rocque: his Life and Work

Although John Rocque claimed the title of Chorographer to King George III in 1761 and despite the fact that his maps of London and its surrounding area are much used by historians, surprisingly little is known of John Rocque either professionally or personally. We know, for instance, that he died in early 1762[1] but not where or when he was born or the year that his family came to settle in England.

It seems probable that his parents were originally French Huguenots who left that country some years after 1685 when Louis XIV revoked the Edict of Nantes which had guaranteed freedom of worship. Their destination was Geneva in Switzerland where they initially brought up their three sons Claude, Bartholomew and John and a daughter Jane. According to John Varley, John was born in 1704 or 1705, and as both Claude and Bartholomew also lived for much of their lives in England, it appears likely that the family came over together from Switzerland a few years after John's birth.

He must have been trained as a surveyor because our first mention of him comes in 1734 when Rocque carries out his first known work, a survey of Richmond House and its gardens. Fortunately for Rocque he had begun his professional career at a particularly favourable moment. The nobility and gentry in the early eighteenth century were displaying great interest in the design and landscaping of their gardens, and the process of enclosures was also gathering speed – both developments calling for accurate surveying. With typical Huguenot energy Rocque combined this work with that of printselling, from 1743 owning a shop on the west side of Piccadilly near Hyde Park Corner. As we also know that at times Rocque employed up to ten draughtsmen and engravers[2], it is evident that his work was recognised as being of a high standard.

In 1737, John Rocque began discussions with the engraver John Pine, regarding the production of a new map of London. After the Great Fire of 1666 the City Corporation had sponsored a new map by John Ogilby and William Morgan which was published in 1676. Measuring 5ft. × 8ft., Ogilby and Morgan's map was invaluable in helping to settle boundary disputes as well as giving an overview of a capital much changed since the 'Copperplate', 'Agas' and Braun and Hogenberg works published in the Tudor period.

However the growth of London had continued unchecked since the survey conducted by Ogilby and Morgan – in particular the westwards expansion out of the city had accelerated – and by the 1730s a new publication was needed: this was what Rocque and Pine set out to fulfil. It should be remembered that something we take for granted today, namely the numbering of buildings, had only begun in the middle of the 1730s and several decades were to pass before this practice became widespread. Rocque's map had a thoroughly practical purpose, that of helping people to find their way around the huge city of London.

John Pine was a well-known engraver who also owned a printshop in St. Martin's Lane near Covent Garden. A friend of William Hogarth, Pine later appeared as the fat friar in that artist's *The Gate of Calais* of 1748 as well as being a governor of Thomas Coram's Foundling Hospital. It seems certain that Pine's social connections must have helped in obtaining the support of the Corporation of London in 1739 for his project with Rocque. The finished map was accordingly dedicated to the Lord Mayor and banker Sir Richard Hoare and also listed the Aldermen by name.

The bulk of the work consisted in a detailed survey of the streets of London, and this was carried out by Rocque. Although he had the use of the improved theodolite recently introduced by the London instrument-maker Jonathan Sisson, it seems that Rocque preferred to draw upon more traditional and less accurate methods. As Professor Richeson has noted[3], eighteenth-century surveyors clung to the use of the chain, a form of elongated ruler for measuring street lengths, and of taking bearings from church steeples. Rocque also trundled around his 'perambulator' or special wheelbarrow whose front wheel had a circumference of 8ft. 3in. or ⅛th of a chain.

Rocque's task took longer than expected, partly as a result of his undertaking a second major work at the same time. This was a survey of the country around London to a distance of 10 miles, a work which was published at intervals between 1744 and 1746. This map of Middlesex and Surrey is itself an excellent source for anyone interested in the eighteenth century. Rocque's map reproduced in this book was finally issued in 1746 and made available to the general public the following year.

Measuring in all some 6½ft. × 13ft., Rocque's publication surveyed London and its neighbouring villages on a scale of 26in. to the mile, more than meeting the demands made of it. Rocque also created, in Philippa Glanville's words, 'a magnificent source for London social history, a vivid picture of the capital some two centuries ago'.[4] It should be stressed however that the map was intended for everyday use: in 1747 an 'Alphabetical Index of the Streets, Squares, Lanes, Alleys etc contained in the Plan . . . with references for the easy finding of the said places' was issued as an accompaniment. The full 24-sheet version cost three guineas, an 8-sheet edition one guinea, and a single sheet copy was priced at 5 shillings[5]. From the scattered evidence we have, it appears that Rocque's map went through three and possibly four editions, confirming that it was indeed the public success which his work deserved.

There is one mystery surrounding the publication of the map. Although John Rocque's name does figure on the finished work, the two names most prominently featured are those of John Pine the engraver and John Tinney the publisher. Strictly speaking therefore, this map should be referred to as 'Pine and Tinney's' rather than 'Rocque's', even though we know that it was the surveyor who was responsible for the bulk of the work. Why did Rocque's name not appear more importantly on the finished work? Ralph Hyde[6] has suggested that Rocque had perhaps overstretched his financial resources and that without the backing of Tinney, a successful printmaker based in Fleet Street, the map would not have been published. But whatever the reason, this map is always described, rightly, as being by John Rocque.

Rocque's career continued to experience its ups and downs. In November 1750 his shop and entire stock in Whitehall, to which he had recently moved, was destroyed in a fire[7]. However, he recovered from this blow and for the rest of his life, Rocque's shop, despite several changes of address, was either in or near the Strand. For several years in the 1750s Rocque was based in Dublin and produced a number of Irish maps. He also published various county maps of parts of England. As for his personal life, we know that Rocque had married Marthe by 1728, and that after her death he took as his second wife in 1751 Mary Anne Bew. There were no children from either marriage.

From the very beginning, Rocque's work had always attracted royal interest and subscriptions, and in 1761 after the accession of George III, Rocque is to be found describing himself as 'Chorographer to His Majesty'. Unfortunately, by this date, John Rocque's health was deteriorating – not helped by the hazard that his surveying work was carried out in all weathers – and he made his will late in 1761. Rocque died on 27th January 1762. His widow Mary Anne continued to run the business at no.438 the Strand for several years, and her publication of John's *The Traveller's Assistant* in 1763, for example, has been called 'the precursor of the present A.B.C. railway and motoring road-books of today.'[8] By 1771 Mary Anne Rocque had moved from the shop and we lose track of her.

After Rocque's death, techniques of mapmaking improved rapidly. For instance, Richard Horwood's work of 1799 shows in careful detail a rapidly growing London, but the portent of the future had come in 1791 when the first sheets of the new Ordnance Survey were issued. Today we have come to expect up-to-date and accurate maps of London, but Rocque's work carried out in the middle of the eighteenth century still retains a distinctive charm and interest as well as telling us much about the city in which this French Huguenot surveyor had lived and worked and of which he knew every street, road and alley.

Notes

[1] John Varley 'John Rocque' *Imago Mundi*, vol. 5, 1948, p. 84.
[2] David Smith *Antique Maps of the British Isles* (1982) p. 39.
[3] A.W. Richeson *English Land Measuring to 1800* (USA, 1966) p. 150.
[4] Philippa Glanville *London in Maps* (1972) p. 37.
[5] H.B. Wheatley 'Rocque's Map of London' *London Topographical Record*, vol. IX, 1914, p. 16.
[6] *The A to Z of Georgian London* (Kent, 1981) vi.
[7] Hugh Phillips 'John Rocque's Career' *London Topographical Record*, vol. XX, 1952, p. 20.
[8] Varley, see above, p. 88.

Suggested Further Reading

The best introduction is Philippa Glanville's *London in Maps* (1972), largely because of its sumptuous examples. Also see James Howgego's *Printed Maps of London c.1553-1850* (Kent, 1978 edition). Harry Margary has republished several old London maps, including John Rocque's as *The A to Z of Georgian London* in 1981 with an introduction by Ralph Hyde. For what little we know about John Rocque, see the articles by John Varley and Hugh Phillips cited in the Notes above.

The Changing Face of LONDON

John Rocque's 1746 Map of London shows a capital which is very clearly defined, stretching some 6 miles from west to east and 3 miles from north to south. Today, however, it is difficult to know where London begins or ends. 250 years ago it was possible to walk right around the circumference of London in an afternoon, a feat impossible now even if the boundaries could be established.

Rocque's London contained a much smaller population than our own. If the present population is, say, 7 million, in the middle of the eighteenth century it was less than one-tenth of that figure. In the intervening period this huge growth has pushed London ever outwards, swallowing up villages such as Islington, Hampstead, Stepney, Knightsbridge and Marylebone which in the 1740s were quite separate from the city. A glance at Rocque's map shows that what we now call 'North London', 'the East End' and 'South London' simply did not exist then. Take the northern districts: our Central Line underground marks the most northern section of Rocque's capital. Fortunately the surveyor did not confine his attention to the inhabited parts of London but also depicted the surrounding fields and gardens which have since been developed. Rocque in fact surveyed London during one of the periodic lulls in building activity, in this instance caused by the collapse of the South Sea Bubble in 1720; not until the 1760s and 1770s did the rate of development pick up again.

It was a London which, within its rigid and hierarchical society, displayed glaring contrasts between rich and poor, a characteristic often noted by foreign visitors to this country. A few individuals tried to improve some of the worst features of every-day life: William Hogarth, for example, with his sequence *The Four Stages of Cruelty* which castigated the treatment of animals, or Thomas Coram who began the Foundling Hospital for abandoned children. Another was Henry Fielding, who wrote in 1753 that

If we were to make a progress through the outskirts of this town (of London) and look into the habitations of the poor, we should there behold such pictures of human misery as must move the compassion of every heart that deserves the name of human.

Most people however regarded the workings of society as somehow immutable and God-given.

The City of London known to Rocque was still largely residential, as it is not today. The seven gates remained in place although they were soon to be removed as constituting an obstruction to traffic. Transport was slow and laborious with the hackney

Henry Fielding (1707-1754), novelist, playwright, magistrate and founder of the Bow Street Runners.

coach ousting the sedan chair. There were over 20,000 horses in the capital and almost as many Thames watermen. It was a London still flooded by cheap gin, a national disease unhindered by legislation until the Act of 1751 imposed heavy duties on corn spirits. But, typically, alongside the squalor of gin-induced poverty were the beautiful new churches raised under the 50 New Churches Act of 1711, a measure passed by a High Church Tory government. It was soon clear that there had been miscalculations:

ye Expence of building with stone, purchasing Scites for Churches, church yards and ministers houses is so very great and does so far exceed the Calculations formerly made that ye Committee Conceive it will be utterly impracticable to build one Half of the Churches at first proposed –[2]

but the twelve which were completed all added to the splendour of London's architecture.

The capital's population remained almost static in the first half of the eighteenth century, rising only from 670,000 in 1700 to 676,000 in 1750, then increasing to 900,000 by 1801. Few streets were lit, there was no income tax or VAT – although there was a window tax – and America was still a colony. Not that the government in London was absolutely secure: a Jacobite rebellion had to be put down in 1745-46.

One way of bringing out the changes which have occurred in London over the last 250 years is to list some of the institutions or places which we take for granted today but which did not exist in the 1750s: in Rocque's time, for example, there were no railway or underground stations; no cinemas or bingo halls; no state schools or town halls; no hotels or restaurants; no garages, petrol stations, car parks or bus stops; no post offices or post boxes; no libraries, museums, concert halls or department stores; no national press or television aerials; no public lavatories; no factories, tower blocks or sports centres; no job centres or doctors' surgeries; and no police stations. There were also very few theatres, bookshops, hospitals, bridges or statues.

On the other hand, several buildings and activities important in the mid-eighteenth century have now disappeared: the City gates, for instance, and the countless tenter grounds used for stretching cloth. Rocque would have been familiar with coffee, chocolate and chop houses whereas we have 'take-aways'. Both pleasure gardens and market gardens, at least in central London, are now unknown, as are watch houses and turnpikes. Rocque's London Bridge obstructed the flow of the Thames, which meant that during especially severe winters the river froze over and

'Frost Fairs' were held. Today the embanked Thames flows at a much faster pace. The docks have been and gone. There has been both loss and gain too as regards the ears and nose. If we have the noisy internal combustion engine to contend with, Rocque had the more pleasant sound of horses' hooves. On the other hand we possess the decent system of sewage and drainage introduced by the Metropolitan Board of Works in the second half of the Victorian period; in this respect Rocque's London hardly bears thinking about.

The major changes to the face of London have derived from new forms of transport. First of all there were the canals, the Grand Junction of 1801 and then the Regent's Canal of 1820 which flowed for nearly nine miles between Paddington and Limehouse. Then came the railway, the big mainline stations which were kept out of central London: Euston, Paddington, Victoria, Waterloo, Liverpool Street and so on. Not only did their construction entail large scale clearances of people – Simon Jenkins[3] gives the figure of 100,000 by the end of the nineteenth century – but also an attendant grubbiness inevitable with the passage of steam engines. Almost at the same time came the Underground with the opening of the first section, between Paddington and Farringdon Street, in 1863. Together, the railway and the Underground led to the growth of the suburbs and a London which would have been inconceivable to Rocque and his contemporaries.

Also in the Victorian era several massive roadbuilding programmes were embarked upon, often as a means of 'social engineering' and involving the extinction of numerous squalid areas of London: New Oxford Street, Victoria Street, Farringdon Road and Street, Shaftesbury Avenue and Charing Cross Road were some of the results. The roads built this century specifically for the motor car, such as the North Circular and the Great West Road, lie well outside the boundaries of Rocque's map.

In the last 50 years there has been the German bombing of the 2nd World War which damaged several areas particularly badly – Stepney, Bermondsey, Rotherhithe, the district around St. Giles, Cripplegate and now the Barbican – but did not alter the pattern of London's streets and buildings. Again, the 'property development' of the 1960s and 1970s certainly transformed the city's skyline but not so much the map of London. The major change has been the continued rapid expansion of the capital's population – as Christopher Hibbert has pointed out[4], an increase greater in the first half of the twentieth century alone than in the previous 2000 years.

But despite the coming of the railway, the

7

underground, the skyscraper and the motor car, there are still many similarities between Rocque's London and our own, enough I think for the modern individual who was suddenly transported back to the London of 250 years ago not to get too lost. Even allowing for all the changes and the expansion, Rocque's map is the first map of our modern London.

Notes

[1] The words of Henry Fielding are quoted from R.W. Malcolmson's *Life and Labour in England 1700-1780* (1981) p. 176.
[2] The 1726 warning of the Commissioners appointed to oversee the building of the 50 New Churches comes from a publication issued by Christ Church, Spitalfields.
[3] Simon Jenkins *Landlords to London* (1975) p. 107.
[4] Christopher Hibbert *London: Biography of a City* (1977 ed.) p. 237.

Suggested Further Reading

Two excellent books on eighteenth-century London which are readily available are Sir John Summerson's *Georgian London* (1978 ed.) and Dorothy George's *London Life in the Eighteenth Century* (1966 ed.). Simon Jenkins' *Landlords to London* (1975) is a valuable discussion of land ownership in London. A lively introduction to the whole period is Roy Porter's *English Society in the Eighteenth Century* (1982).

Good general histories of London are: S.E. Rasmussen *London: the Unique City* (USA, 1982 ed.), Christopher Hibbert *London: Biography of a City* (1977 ed.) and Felix Barker and Peter Jackson *London, 2000 Years of a City* (1984 ed.) which is very well illustrated.

One of the best introductions to the subject comes from the writings of seventeenth- and eighteenth-century observers, amongst them the diaries of Samuel Pepys and John Evelyn, selections of which are available in paperback; James Boswell's *London Journal*; the *London Spy* of Ned Ward; Daniel Defoe's works, particularly *Moll Flanders, A Tour Through The Whole Island of Great Britain* and *A Journal of the Plague Year*; John Wesley's *Journal* – and look at any of the work of William Hogarth.

Note Before Looking At The Maps

John Rocque's surveying of London in the 1730s and 1740s was thorough and detailed, but his work was not completely accurate. In other words, the maps of Rocque's London and of our own do not always provide a perfect fit.

Rocque divided up his map of London into 24 sections, and within each of them he made a grid around the outside. I have used this numbering in order to help readers find items mentioned in the commentary: the first number refers to the vertical scale, the second figure to the horizontal.

Rocque and his engraver John Pine obtained City of London support for their project. The numbers which appear in the City sections of Rocque's map refer to the wards represented by the Aldermen. The word 'City' describes the actual City of London bounded by the wall, the word 'city', London as a whole.

A contracted Sketch of the PLAN of LONDON &c. printed on 24 Sheets of Imperial Paper, to shew the General Appearance of the Whole; for the Use of those who bind it in a Book, and for the better comprehending the Divisions mentioned in the Index.

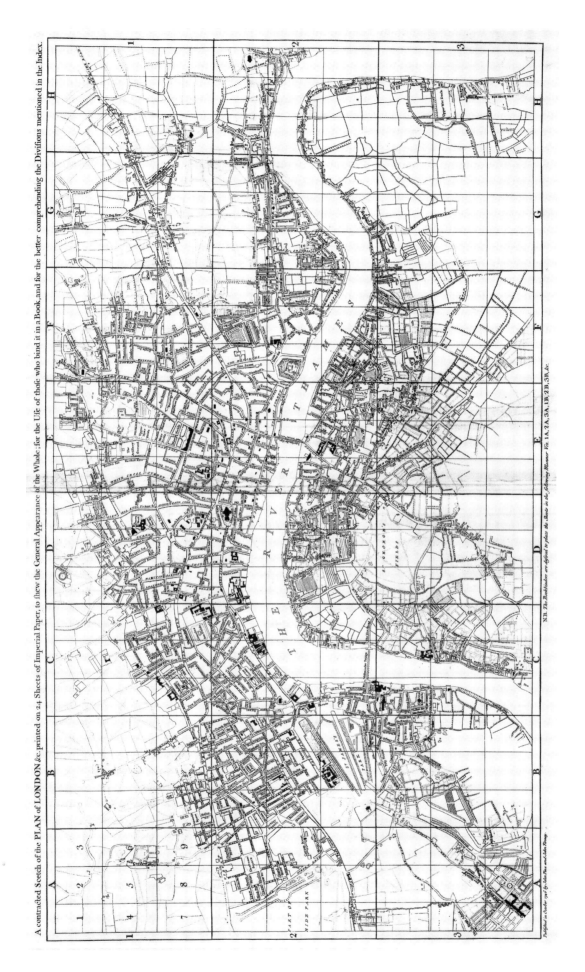

N.B. The Bookbinder are desired to place the Sheets in the following Manner Viz. 1A, 2A, 3A, 1B, 2B, 3B, &c.

Published in October 1746 by John Pine and John Tinney.

9

Marylebone

This top left-hand corner of John Rocque's map shows the area which today would be loosely referred to as Marylebone. In the 1740s it was still a village some way from London, but the spread of development can just be seen pushing into the bottom edge (13/9). Rocque called it 'Marybone'; the name derives from the church of St. Mary (7/6) that had once been on the banks of the

William Hogarth (1697-1764) whose sequences such as *The Harlot's Progress*, *The Rake's Progress* and *Industry and Idleness* illuminate eighteenth-century London life.

river Tyburn which flows through the district: hence St. Mary le Burn and finally Marylebone.

The St. Mary's shown by Rocque was the centre of the village and dated back to around 1400. Lying outside London the church was much favoured as the venue for dubious or illicit marriages – in Hogarth's *The Rake's Progress* Tom weds the elderly but rich spinster here. Six years after Hogarth's painting a new and larger church was erected further up the High Street in 1740. This building's churchyard has survived today as a Garden of Rest just at the back of the present and more grandiose St. Mary's of 1817, constructed on a much larger scale because of Marylebone's expanding population in the early nineteenth century. The 'Marybone Burying Ground' (9/5) was used by the new church of St. George's, Hanover Square until the mid-Victorian period: it is now in part Paddington Street Gardens.

At the heart of this section of Rocque's map are the 'Marybone Gardens' (7/7). In the seventeenth century a tavern called the Rose of Normandy had been built in Marylebone High Street, its name being a recognition of the little group of Huguenot immigrants from France who had settled nearby. At the back of the tavern were some bowling-greens and gardens which had been visited by Pepys in May 1668 together with several of his lady friends: 'Then we abroad to Marrowbone, and there walked in the garden; the first time I ever was there, and a pretty place it is.' He recorded in his *Diary* that his party had stayed eating and drinking until 9 o'clock in the evening.

In the 1730s the proprietor of the Rose of Normandy, David Gough, decided to redesign the Gardens on a much grander scale, installing an orchestra and offering his patrons food, drink, fireworks, bowls and a variety of walks much favoured by lovers – all this for an entrance fee of 6d. The Gardens quickly established a strong musical tradition, often playing pieces by Handel. On one occasion Handel himself visited the Gardens with an old clergyman as company. The parson heard some of the music performed and turning to Handel remarked 'It is not worth listening to; it is very poor stuff.' 'You are right,' replied the composer, 'I thought so myself when I had finished it.' After seeing the clergyman's evident embarrassment, Handel sought to set him at his ease again by saying that his opinion was as correct as it had been honest.

In 1767 the then proprietor went bankrupt because of an especially rainy season which had kept away the customers, and the Marylebone Gardens closed down soon after. Like much of the surrounding neighbourhood they were built over in the late eighteenth century. However the Rose of Normandy survived until after the 2nd World War, and although demolished in 1956 the frontage of the pub still frames the businesses now stationed at nos. 32-33 Marylebone High Street.

The road by which visitors reached the Gardens was the thin and curving 'Marybone Lane' which today still retains these characteristics, running across Wigmore Row, now Wigmore Street (12/8). The little patch of building in this corner had been sponsored in the first decades of the century by Robert Harley, 1st Earl of Oxford, who owned the land. Although leaving behind several permanent reminders of his name – for instance in Oxford Street and Harley Street – he had been temporarily brought up short by the collapse of the South Sea Bubble in the autumn of 1720 and further development was suspended until after Rocque had finished his survey.

The Oxford Chapel (13/9), now St. Peter's, had been finished between 1722 and 1724. Intended to minister to the spiritual welfare of 'the Inhabitants of the new Buildings in Marybone Fields', the church was designed by Harley himself and executed under the supervision of the architect James Gibbs, also engaged at the time on his most famous church of St. Martin-in-the-Fields. The Oxford Chapel was renamed St. Peter's in 1832 and is now the home of the London Institute for Contemporary Christianity.

Apart from this minor development Rocque's map is dominated by fields: the only other major places he shows are Daget's Farm (4/4) and the Jew's Harp House (3/6), another eighteenth-century pleasure resort. These Marylebone Fields were suitable for several other activities. One was the holding of duels, being a suitable distance from London to ensure that the authorities did not interfere. Secondly, the fields were the haunt of highwaymen, preying on travellers as

they straggled into the capital. In John Gay's play *The Beggar's Opera* of 1728, Macheath and his gang often lurk here. In real life Dick Turpin is supposed to have frequented the fields also, and certainly the proprietors of the Marylebone Gardens had to provide armed guards for the escort of revellers back to town at night.

Marylebone Fields were also the location for sporting events, including dog-fights. The playwright and poet John Gay wrote:

Both Hockley-hole and Marybone
The combats of my dog have known.

A few years after Rocque's survey the first Lord's Cricket Ground was laid down in what is now Dorset Square (see the top left-hand corner of the modern map). In 1786 members of the White Conduit Club of Islington decided to find new premises and therefore delegated a certain Thomas Lord, wine merchant and slow bowler, to carry out their wishes. Lord leased a field in Marylebone and almost single-handedly got the ground in shape for the summer of 1787: the first match took place here between Middlesex and Essex for a stake of 200 guineas on May 31st and June 1st 1787. Within a few months the Marylebone Cricket Club (MCC) was founded. By 1800 the little ground was attracting crowds of up to 5,000 people and Lord moved to the more spacious North Bank in Regent's Park before settling the venue in St. John's Wood in 1814, its present site.

Mention of Regent's Park provides a reminder that of Rocque's Marylebone Fields, this is all that has survived. Originally one of Henry VIII's hunting parks, the area was redesigned by the Prince Regent's personal architect John Nash in the early nineteenth century. He surrounded the park with magnificent terraces of houses, laid out the canal which runs around the northern perimeter, but failed to build the proposed royal palace.

The rest of Rocque's fields have disappeared, leaving only fragments in the form of Manchester, Portman, Montagu and Bryanston Squares. It was only a matter of time before the district was developed. In 1757 the road we now call Marylebone Road was opened as part of the 'New Road from Paddington to Islington', and under this stimulus landowners such as the Portmans set out to profit from their estates. The name of many of the squares and roads originate either in property held elsewhere by the Portmans, such as at Bryanston in Dorset, or from individuals known to them: the Baker family were their business partners.

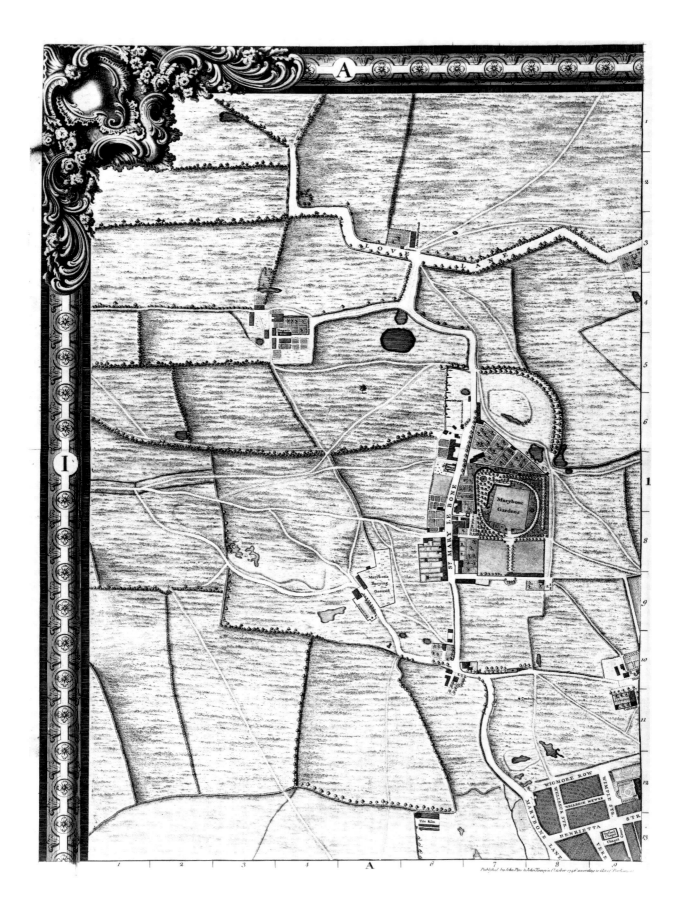

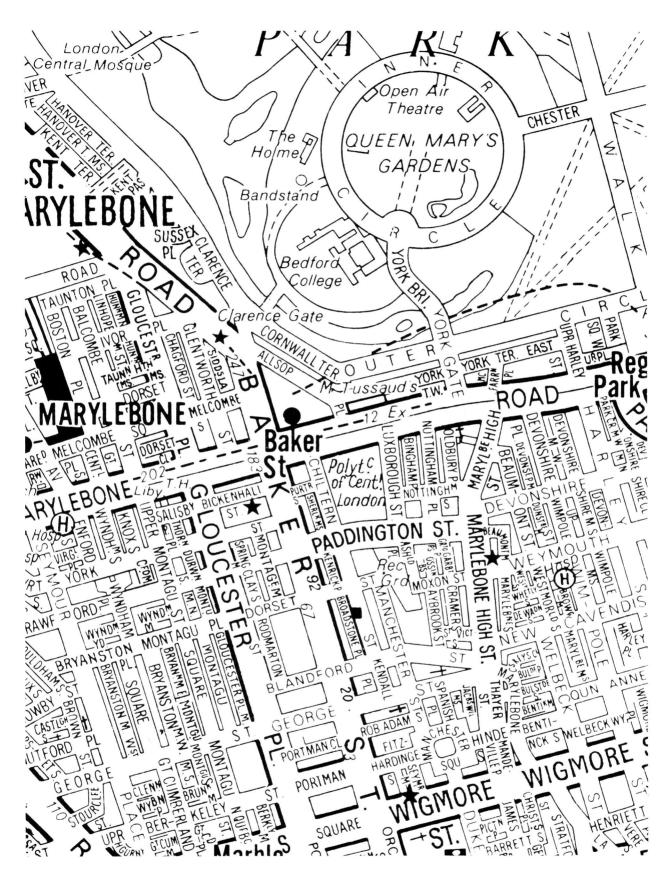

Hyde Park and Mayfair

The contours of John Rocque's map of Hyde Park and Mayfair have changed little when compared with today. Knightsbridge (12/2), down at the bottom, has been developed since the 1740s, but the major roads shown have retained their position if not their names: Tiburn Road (1/6) is now Oxford Street, Tiburn Lane (4/3) is Park Lane, Knightsbridge and Piccadilly still cross the southern half of our modern map, and even the paths of what became Sloane Street and Grosvenor Road can be glimpsed on Rocque's survey.

Mayfair itself by the 1740s was in the final throes of development – evidence of continuing building work is seen beside Chesterfield House (8/7). Already the area was highly favoured by the wealthy and fashionable who had moved out of the crowded and dirty City towards the open spaces lying to the west, a migration with obvious financial benefit to those landowners whose estates were located there. In this case it was the Grosvenors and the Berkeleys: hence Grosvenor Square (4/6) and Berkeley Square (5/9).

One attraction of Mayfair was clearly Hyde Park, another of Henry VIII's hunting parks which, although sold off to private buyers during the Commonwealth, had been restored to public use by Charles II after the Restoration. The brick wall which had once surrounded the park had been removed by 1726, thus allowing Londoners the opportunity to roam its acres. The inhabitants of the neighbourhood exercised their horses here and Rocque's The King's Old Road to Kensington (11/3) became the fashionable parade of Rotten Row. The Serpentine had been laid out in 1733 by George II's Queen Caroline, offering the chance of swimming in the summer and skating during the winter. However like so many outlying districts of London, Hyde Park was frequented by duellists and also by highwaymen; at night, bells would be rung at the various gates in order to allow travellers to gather together in numbers.

But if Hyde Park was the positive side of Mayfair, there were still two significant objections to living here.

The first is clearly shown by Rocque: the triangular gallows at Tyburn (2/1). Ever since the twelfth century Tyburn had been despatching wrongdoers, usually after a 3-mile and 2-hour cart-ride from Newgate prison, often in batches and always in front of huge crowds. In Rocque's day a certain Mother Proctor erected her 'Pews' for spectators and most of the city's apprentices would take the afternoon off on the eight hanging days each year. In 1664 Samuel Pepys had come here in order to see a former acquaintance of his hanged for robbery, paying 1/- for the dubious privilege of standing on the wheel of a cart and obtaining a better view. In May 1763 it was James Boswell's turn, come to see the execution of the highwayman Paul Lewis:

I took Captain Temple with me, and he and I got upon a scaffold very near the fatal tree, so that we could clearly see the dismal scene. There was a most prodigious crowd of spectators. I was most terribly shocked, and thrown into a very deep melancholy.

200,000 people are thought to have attended when the highwayman Jack Sheppard was hanged in 1724, and the orgiastic nature of the proceedings is suggested by the penultimate plate in Hogarth's *Industry and Idleness* series. After the execution the crowd would fight over the corpse: family and friends wanted to bury it decently, the authorities to convey it to the Surgeon's Hall for anatomical reasons. Not surprisingly the well-connected new residents of Mayfair like the Earl of Chesterfield, who moved here in 1733, campaigned for Tyburn to be ended. Successfully too: from 1783 public hangings took place outside Newgate prison. The name Tyburn was soon obliterated from the adjoining Street and Lane, being replaced by Oxford (the Earl of) and Park (after Hyde Park).

The second drawback had actually given the area its name: every May a fair had been held in the vicinity (9/8). Like Tyburn this Mayfair had attracted the rowdy and the drunk, as is clear from Ned Ward's withering description:

I never in all my life saw such a number of lazy-look'd rascals, and so hateful a throng of beggarly, sluttish strumpets, who were a scandal to the Creation, mere antidotes against lechery, and enemies to cleanliness.

This fair was ended during the course of the eighteenth century, its only indirect legacy being today's Shepherd Market, first introduced by a Mr. Edward Shepherd in the 1730s (8/9).

But if the wealthy had removed the gallows and the fair, they did need some facilities of their own, particularly a place in which to worship. St. George's in Hanover Square was too small and therefore in 1730 Grosvenor Chapel (6/6) was opened. Ann Callender has observed of it that

During the London season from December to May, Grosvenor Chapel was very much the House of Lords at prayer.[1]

Beautifully restored, it is still on this site today. A more infamous chapel was the Mayfair chapel (8/8), run in the middle of the eighteenth century by a Reverend Keith who operated as a marriage broker: in some years Keith married up to 6,000 couples here, which is about twenty each and every day of the week. The Marriage Act of 1753 ended Keith's activities and he subsequently died in Fleet prison.

Perhaps the most famous resident of Mayfair at the time of Rocque's survey was not in fact a member of the aristocracy but the musician George Frederick Handel who lived at no.25 Brook Street (2/9) between 1724 and his death in 1759. Naturalised as a British subject in 1726, Handel must have been composing his *Messiah* in the music room on the 1st floor at the time when

Rocque was wandering the streets outside with his 'perambulator'.

Rocque's Hyde Park Corner (11/6) is not the congested roundabout of today but he would have known the famous coaching inn called the Hercules Pillars, its odd name being explained by its site at the western limit of London just like the rocks guarding the entrance to the Mediterranean. In Henry Fielding's *Tom Jones* of 1749 Squire Western and his entourage stay here. Today it has been replaced by the Duke of Wellington's former residence Apsley House. When built it was sometimes referred to as No.1, London, and one can see why from Rocque's map: it would have been the first substantial house encountered by a traveller from the West country.

Constitution Hill (12/9) can be seen down in the corner but it did not then fringe Buckingham Palace which in the 1740s was still Buckingham House. Further along to the west is now Belgravia, discussed in the next section. St. George's Hospital (12/5) had been founded here in 1733 after a split from the Westminster Hospital; today it is an empty shell awaiting development.

Of the major changes since Rocque's day, 'Where Soldiers are shot' (12/1) is now just beside our Speakers' Corner, near to Marble Arch which was placed here in 1851 after it was discovered that the state coach was too large to drive underneath and therefore it had to be removed from its original position outside Buckingham Palace. Our Edgware Road can just be made out on Rocque's map (1/1): in the 1740s it led to the pleasant little village of Paddington with its St. Mary's church in the middle of Paddington Green. The eloping couple William Hogarth and Jane Thornhill had come here in 1729 in order to get married; fortunately for them, Hogarth's father-in-law was eventually reconciled to the match.

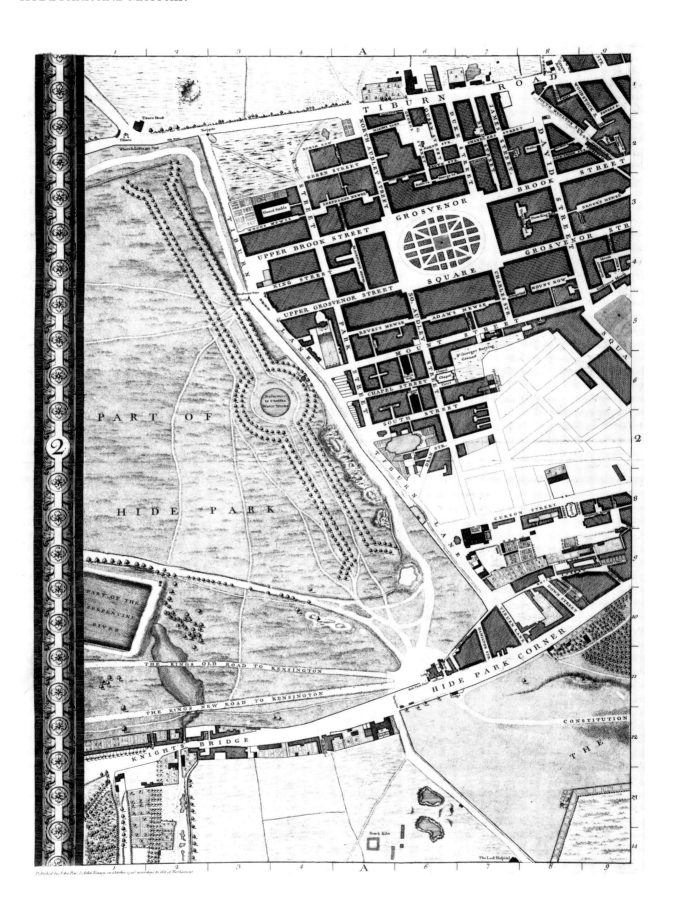

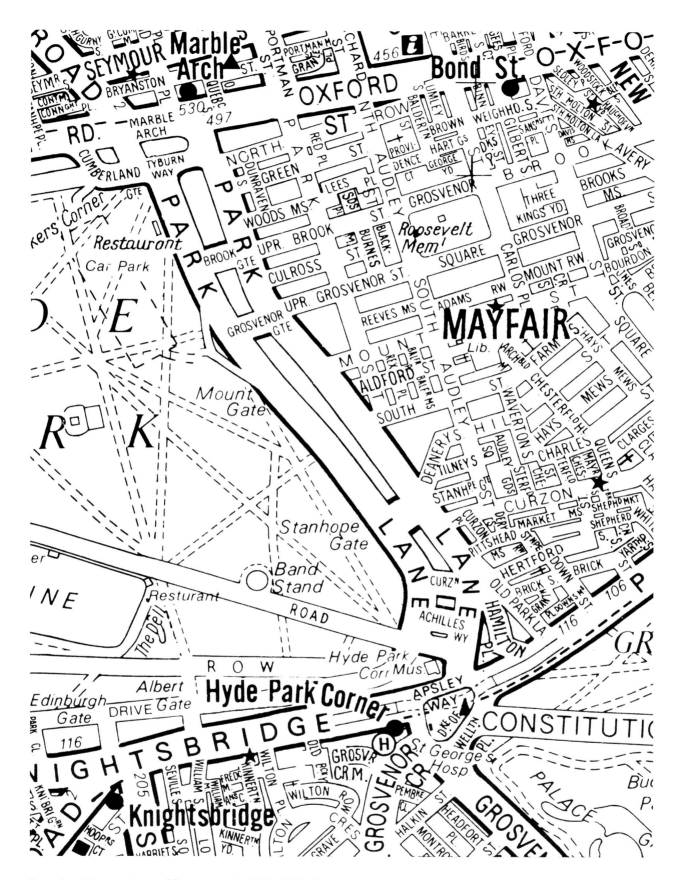

Reproduced by permission of Geographers' A-Z Map Co Ltd.

Belgravia and Chelsea

This is another section of Rocque's map where one has to work hard to make connections between his day and ours. Today the area is Belgravia and Chelsea – but 250 years ago Belgravia did not exist and Chelsea was an outlying village several miles from London, which was precisely the reason its most famous past resident, Sir Thomas More, had moved there in about 1520 whilst still Chancellor of the Exchequer. As late as 1711 Jonathan Swift took lodgings at Chelsea because he enjoyed the stroll into London. Only the King's Road, winding its way down from the top eastern corner and still in the 1740s a private thoroughfare reserved for the use of the royal family, has retained its name since Rocque's day.

The reason for this tardy development of the northern section of the map was the district's wet and swampy character. However in the course of the first half of the nineteenth century the fortuitous position of his land near the new royal residence of Buckingham Palace prompted the then Duke of Westminster to develop his estate under the supervision of the builder Thomas Cubitt. In the same period of the 1820s Cubitt was also engaged on the construction of St. Katharine's Dock beside the Tower of London, and he decided to float the rubble from this excavation down the Thames in barges and use it here as ballast. The name 'Belgravia' came from that of the village in one of the Westminster family's other estates in Cheshire, and the centrepieces of this London project were Belgrave Square and Eaton Square, both of which have remained virtually intact to this day.

The path running down from the top of this map, at one point becoming extraordinarly twisted, is now Sloane Street, named after the physician and book collector Sir Hans Sloane, a longstanding resident of Chelsea. Sloane, whose patients had included Samuel Pepys and Queen Anne, had been a patron of the Chelsea Physic Garden when it opened in 1673, just to the west of this map, and a statue of him erected in 1737 still stands in the middle of the garden. He died at the Manor House, Chelsea in 1753 aged 92. Apart from Sloane's Manor House, the other aristocratic dwelling in the neighbourhood was Chelsea House (9/1) – residence throughout the eighteenth century of the Cadogan family – hence the nearby Square, Place, Lane and Gardens of the same name in the modern map.

The river Thames flows just past the bottom of this map, explaining why Chelsea was originally a fishermen's village. However its sense of rural splendour only a few miles from the City and Westminster soon enticed other institutions to establish themselves here, and Rocque shows two of the most famous, the Chelsea College or Hospital (12/3) and next to it the famous Ranelagh Gardens (12/5).

The former was founded by Charles II – reputedly acting on the suggestion of his mistress Nell Gwyn – in order to look after the retired or injured members of the royal bodyguard. The designs were drawn up by the diarist John Evelyn; the young Nicholas Hawksmoor was paid 10/- 'for drawing designs of ye hospitall'; and Sir Christopher Wren was entrusted with the building of 'The Hospital of Maymed Soldiers'. The first residents or 'Chelsea Pensioners' were admitted in 1689. By Rocque's day admission was restricted to those 'maimed and disabled in the Service of the Crown, or that hath served the Crown twenty years'; the running costs of the Hospital were met by stopping 'one Day's pay of each Officer, and of each common Soldier' in the army each year.

The Hospital also held musical events in the eighteenth century. John Ashton in his *Social Life in the Reign of Queen Anne* prints a notice of 1702 advertising a concert to be given here by 'The Ladies' consort of Musick' which ends: 'Notice that the Moon will shine, the Tide serve, and a Guard placed from the College to St. James's Park for the safe return of the Ladies.' Fortunately much of Wren's Chelsea Hospital has survived.

On the east side of the Hospital lived Sir Robert

Ranelagh Gardens in Chelsea, an illustration which brings out the exotic setting of this pleasure garden.

Walpole, the Whig politician, who bought his house here in 1722 for the sum of £1,000. Walpole later became the country's first Prime Minister and moved to no.10 Downing Street, but he was invariably accused of greed and bribery: in *The Beggar's Opera* of 1728 the highwayman Macheath says of Peachum, the character taken by audiences to be a representation of Walpole, that 'he's a good honest kind of fellow and one of us'. There is now a Walpole Street in Chelsea.

Bordering on the Chelsea Hospital were the Ranelagh Gardens (12/5), the most fashionable of all the numerous Georgian pleasure gardens. Opened in 1742, its entrance fee of 2/6d doubtless excluded the less prosperous. Chelsea Pensioners from the Hospital often served as guards and escorts. The Gardens appear in many novels and diaries of the time – Oliver Goldsmith for example in his *The Vicar of Wakefield* of 1764 refers to it disparagingly as being a market for wives – if only because its decor included a Rotunda or 'Musick Theatre', Chinese Gardens and a massive central fireplace. Horace Walpole, son of Sir Robert, noted in 1744 regarding its fashionableness that 'you can't set your foot (in Ranelagh) without treading on a Prince of Wales or a Duke of Cumberland'.[2] Five years later Walpole is to be found enthusing over Ranelagh's celebration of the recent peace treaty signed with France: 'nothing in a fairy tale ever surpassed it'. He went on to describe the orchestra playing from within a gondola, the shops filled with Dresden china, the brilliantly illuminated amphitheatre, the orange-trees filled with lamps, the festoons of natural flowers;

There were booths for tea and wine, gaming-tables and dancing, and about two thousand persons. In short, it pleased me more than anything I ever saw.

Ranelagh Gardens eventually closed down in the early nineteenth century and its site is now occupied in part by Chelsea Barracks. Another well-known resort, only a few hundred yards away, was the Chelsea Bun House which was opened in the late seventeenth century near Jew's Row (10/3), our Pimlico Road. Specialising in Chelsea Buns sold on Good Fridays, so popular that crowds of many thousand would besiege the small shop, the Bun House remained in vogue throughout the Georgian period. However there was once a dissatisfied customer; Jonathan Swift recorded in the May 1711 entry of his *Journal to Stella* that he bought 'one (bun) today in my walk; it cost me a penny; it was stale and I did not like it'. The Chelsea Bun House closed down in 1839 but its existence is commemorated by our Bunhouse Place just to the north of Pimlico Road.

On the right of Rocque's map can be seen a stretch of water crossed by Chelsea Bridge (9/8), now Ebury Bridge. Fed by the Thames, this passage proved vital to the development of the area: in 1823 it was turned into the Grosvenor Canal and used by Thomas Cubitt for conveying the materials essential to his Belgravia and Pimlico works. The Chelsea Water Works (13/7) have been replaced by the Western Pumping Station built by Sir Joseph Bazalgette between 1872 and 1875. Rocque's Neat Houses (10/8) derive their name from the word 'Neyte' meaning a small island, yet another indication of this area's riverside associations.

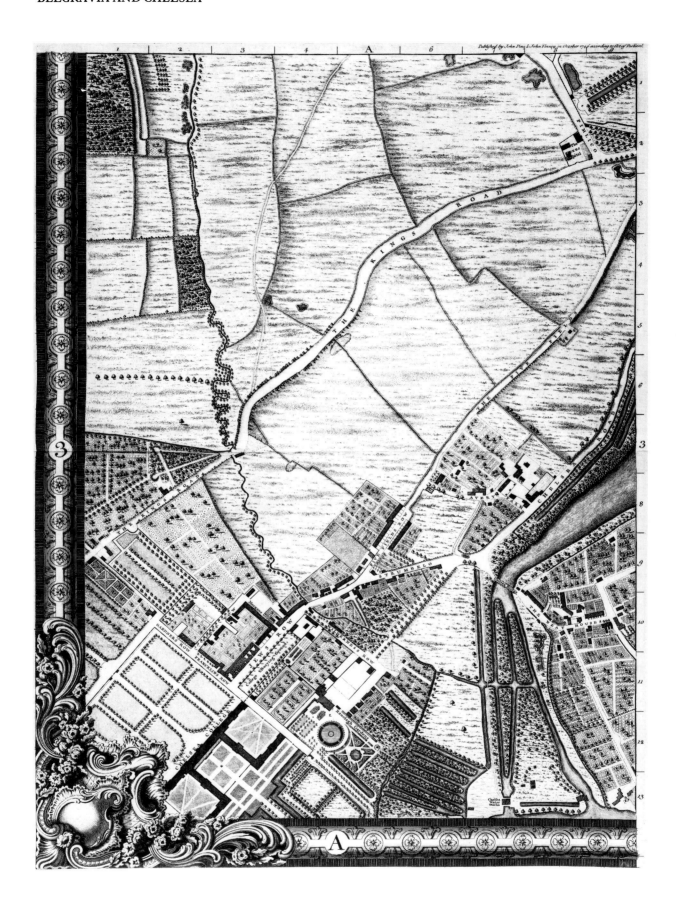

Reproduced by permission of Geographers' A-Z Map Co Ltd.

Fitzrovia

Today this area is usually known as 'Fitzrovia', primarily because of Fitzroy Square built on Charles Fitzroy's land towards the end of the eighteenth century, several decades after John Rocque's survey. It has also been called 'North Soho' and even 'London's Latin Quarter'.

However 250 years ago the only development which had taken place centred on Cavendish Square (12/1) – not fully completed as Rocque's sketchy outline suggests – and Soho Square (13/8). The latter had been a fashionable address ever since the Restoration of 1660, even though one of its residents, the Duke of Monmouth, had come to grief in 1685 when his rebellion against James II was crushed at the Battle of Sedgemoor. Before that the fields of Soho had been another of Henry VIII's hunting grounds, giving rise to the district's name: 'So-ho' was an old hunting cry. Soho Square had once been known as King Square after Charles II, a statue of whom still stands in the middle of the gardens.

But by Rocque's day Soho was rapidly losing its aristocratic pretensions as the powerful and wealthy moved ever westwards. One reason for their migration from this neighbourhood was the deterioration of St. Giles – Rocque shows the High Street (13/10) – into one of the most squalid parts of London. The plague of 1665 was supposed to have started here, and every year saw an annual influx of unskilled Irish labourers. Today St. Giles is dominated by Centrepoint and by the continuous flow of traffic along the two Victorian roads intended to clear away some of the slums: Charing Cross Road which replaced Hog Lane (13/9) and New Oxford Street which subsumed Banbridge Street (12/10). One reminder of the past is the Catholic church of St. Patrick's in Soho Square which was built for the poorer Irish inhabitants, having started in 1792 as 'Father O'Leary's Chapel'. Diagonally across the square stands a French church, indicating that Soho was the site of a substantial Huguenot community after 1685.

Oxford Street (13/4) had only recently acquired this name, having been in turn 'The Way to Uxbridge' and Tyburn road. In Rocque's day Oxford Street was far from being our own bright shopping precinct; one of his contemporaries described it as

a deep hollow road, and full of sloughs, with here and there a ragged house, the lurking-place of cut-throats; insomuch that I never was taken that way by night in my hackney-coach to a worthy uncle, who gave me lodgings in his house in George Street, but I went in dread the whole way.

Angel Hill (now Dean Street), Wardour Street (13/7) and Berwick Street (13/6) lead off Oxford Street to the south. To the north is Oxford Market (12/4) which was in business from 1721 until 1876, but today survives only in the name Market Place.

The centrepiece of this development was to have been Cavendish Square (12/1), named, like so many other roads and streets in this vicinity, after Robert Harley, the 1st Earl of Oxford, and his family; in Simon Jenkins' words,

he produced Harley, Mortimer, Wigmore and de Vere Streets named after himself and his various titles; Cavendish Square and Henrietta Street after his wife; Holles and Wimpole Streets after his father-in-law and the latter's country seat; and Margaret Street after his only daughter and heiress. Later his mother-in-law was to be commemorated in no uncertain manner elsewhere on the estate. She had been the daughter of the Duke of Newcastle, who was also Viscount Mansfield and Baron Ogle, and she was the heiress of the villages of Welbeck, Clipstone and Carburton in Nottinghamshire and Bolsover in Derbyshire.[3]

The Harley estate was seen as the Tory rival to the Whig development around Hanover Square on the other side of Oxford Street.

Cavendish Square was never as splendid a unity as anticipated. The collapse of the South Sea Bubble in 1720 had hindered further expansion here, and although houses around the square were inhabited from 1724, the northern side was still not completed by the 1740s. Intended for the town dwelling of the Duke of Chandos (hence our Chandos Street), if it had come to fruition the Duke would have been able to walk from here to his palace at Edgware without stepping off his own land. But the house was never built and to this day Cavendish Square still retains a rather fragmented character; it was a failure which proved, as Sir John Summerson has noted,

that members of the aristocracy were not interested in their town houses to anything like the extent that they were in their country dwellings.[4]

Apart from the new buildings and streets around Cavendish Square, Rocque's map of London north of Oxford Street is largely made up of fields and ponds. Tottenham Court Road (9/7) remains of course, but whereas 250 years ago it offered a lonely and dangerous passage before becoming the Road to Highgate, today it is always full of traffic forging a way between crowded pavements and department stores. Hogarth's painting of 1746 called *The March to Finchley* is set in this area and shows the hills of Hampstead and Highgate receding into the far distance.

However, one institution marked by Rocque remains to this day: the Middlesex Hospital (10/8) which was founded in Windmill Street in 1745 for the sick, the lame and lying-in married women. That it is present in Rocque's map, published in 1746, demonstrates the thoroughness with which he tried to update his survey. In 1756 the Middlesex moved to its present site in Mortimer Street. The Green Lane (7/4) meandering down from the north is now Cleveland Street, but of our Charlotte, Goodge or Gower Streets there is not even a hint. University College, London which sits in the north-east corner of the modern map was not founded until 1828.

The explanation of Fitzrovia's development in the late eighteenth century underlines once more the importance of roads and transport. The New Road – today's Marylebone and Euston Roads – was opened in 1757 with the aim of keeping the cattle on their way to Smithfield out of central and residential London. The local landowner Charles Fitzroy, whose father had been an illegitimate child of Charles II just like the Duke of Monmouth, sought to seize the opportunities which were thus offered to his estate. He hired the famous architectural brothers, the Adams, to work on his Fitzroy Square project, and evidence of their elegant style survives to this day – but Fitzroy was too late. The westwards shift of the affluent had already passed by this district, attracted instead to Mayfair. In the early nineteenth century it was an address in Belgravia which was much coveted.

Fitzroy's estate lost its remaining social cachet when the substantial houses were split up into multiple dwellings, ideal for small businesses such as furniture and cabinet-making. Both Heal's and Maples began here, their enormous stores still lining Tottenham Court Road. Artists too found it a congenial location: John Constable lived at no.76 Charlotte Street between 1822 and 1837. Even then this north side of London had been little developed – Constable enjoyed a view of the Hampstead Hills.

That Fitzrovia declined in status must have been even more galling when the two estates on either side prospered, the Portmans to the west and the Bedfords to the east. Bedford Square was built at the same time as Fitzroy Square, on roughly the site of the Timber Yard (10/9) shown by Rocque, but the Bedford estate's technique of staggering the leases and the gates strategically placed to ensure its residents' privacy meant that it did not suffer the same fate as Fitzroy Square.

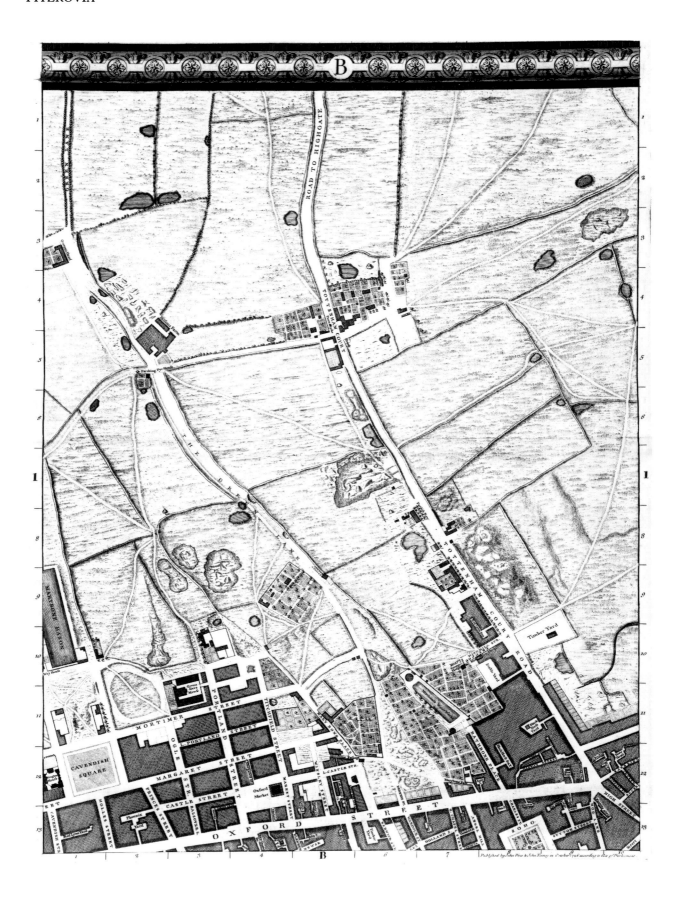

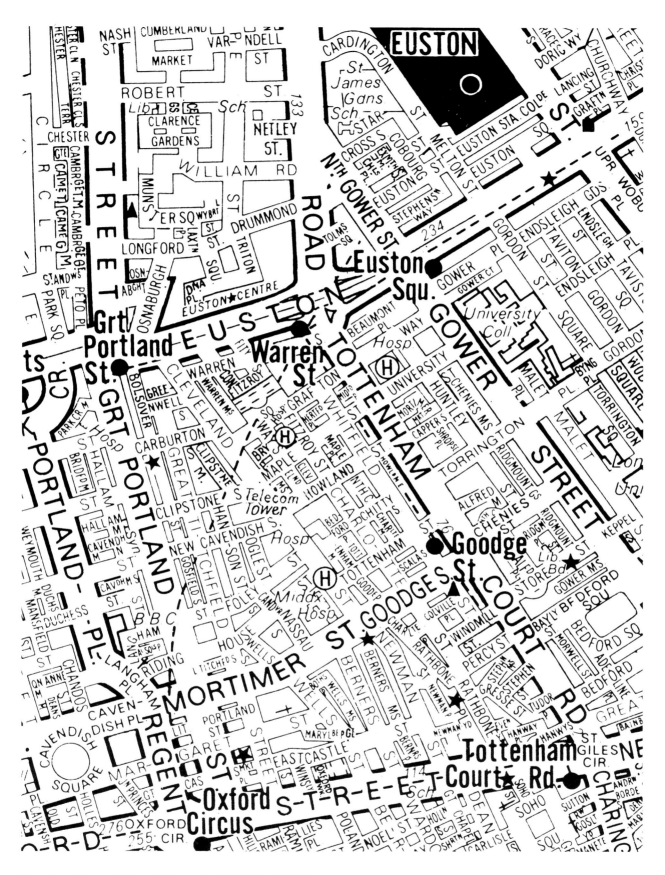

Reproduced by permission of Geographers' A-Z Map Co Ltd.

Piccadilly and St. James's

Unlike some of John Rocque's other sections, the similarities between this area as it was 250 years ago and as it is today are apparent. The reason for this continuity is that Piccadilly has always been a major thoroughfare – even in the sixteenth century when it was called 'The Way to Redinge' – and by the next century was also attracting those members of the nobility who wished to live outside but close to the City. Thus by the 1740s, the area had already been substantially developed. Incidentally, it was a district which Rocque himself would have known well: for several years until 1749 he owned a printshop beside White Horse Street (9/1).

In the middle of Rocque's map sits the smart St. James's Square (8/7), laid out in the 1660s and a symbol of this neighbourhood's fashionableness. In his guide to London, David Piper has pointed out that in 1721 the square's residents numbered some six Dukes and seven Earls[5]: in 1738, when Rocque was engaged on his survey, the future George III was born here. The inhabitants naturally had their own church, St. James's Piccadilly (6/6), built by Wren between 1676 and 1684 and the most well-connected church of the eighteenth century, and also their own club: White's was on the east side of St. James's Street (8/4). Sir Robert Walpole had moved into 5 Arlington Street (8/3) in 1742 after he resigned as Prime Minister, living there with his writer son Horace. By contrast, the young and unknown Samuel Johnson had spent one night in the late 1730s walking around and around St. James's Square with a friend 'for want of a lodging'[6].

Piccadilly itself is supposed to have derived its name from the 'Pikkadille' or ruff collar introduced by a Mr. Baker who had lived in the vicinity during the previous century. After the Restoration of 1660, several returning Royalist exiles acquired land here and thus some of the streets still bear their names: Albemarle, Dover, Burlington. Some of them also built huge mansions, and although Clarendon House had been demolished by the 1740s, Devonshire House (8/3) and Burlington House (6/4) had survived, the latter in parts

still with us as the home of the Royal Academy. The roads to the north of Piccadilly had been slow in their development, explained by the damp and marshy nature of the surroundings, and not until Sir Thomas Bond had bought the land did building work commence in earnest.

Like St. James's Square, the area between Piccadilly and Oxford Street – just off the northern edge of Rocque's map – was highly fashionable, which in turn led to the inevitable laying out of squares: Berkeley to the left (5/1) and Hanover at the top (2/2). The name of the latter confirms that this neighbourhood was something of a Whig enclave, the party regarded as stalwart supporters of the Georges from Hanover. Just as St. James's Square boasted its own church, dwellers in Hanover Square used St. George's (3/3), completed in 1724. George Frederick Handel was a churchwarden here at the time of Rocque's survey and maintained his own pew. Golden Square (4/5) was never as up-market as its two neighbours. The area as a whole was still residential: the shops in New and Old Bond Street, for example, had not yet pushed out the inhabitants.

The attractions of Piccadilly and St. James's were considerably enhanced by the proximity of Green Park and St. James's Park. Although the former was and still is rather flat and featureless, it did at least provide a break within the rush of building spreading westwards. To the south of it is the tree-lined Mall, so called because of Charles II's fondness for playing 'pell-mell' or croquet here. Not only had Charles laid out the four lines of trees in St. James's Park but he also installed his mistress Nell Gwyn nearby, as the diarist John Evelyn noted in March 1671 when he and Charles met 'Mrs. Nellie as they cal'd an impudent Comedian, she looking out of her Garden on a Tarrace at the top of the Wall . . . I was heartily sorry at this scene.' It does not appear to have worried Charles that his father had set off from St. James's Palace (10/5) on his walk across the park to his execution at Whitehall on January 30th, 1649.

St. James's Park had been named after Charles II's

St. James's Park in the late eighteenth century; Buckingham House is at the rear.

grandfather, but it was Charles who had hired the celebrated French gardener Le Nôtre to landscape it. By the early eighteenth century it was a fashionable spot at which the fashionable could parade, show off their new clothes and gossip. Like Green Park it was open to the public: Defoe's Moll Flanders steals a gold watch from a little child in the park and James Boswell in 1763 picked up a 17-year-old prostitute here – 'Poor being, she has a sad time of it!' The line of trees along the bottom of the park now marks our Birdcage Walk but in the 1740s it was still a private path reserved for the royal family. Its present name derived from the aviary kept here by James I, but one can also see a cockpit nearby (14/9). Buckingham House (13/2) at the west end of St. James's Park was still that and not a Palace until the 1820s when it was converted by George IV's architect John Nash.

Nash was responsible for several major changes in this area, amongst them Carlton House Terrace which now lies between Pall Mall and the Mall but more significantly for Regent Street. Built in the 1810s, Nash constructed it so as to wipe out many of the less reputable streets and alleys fringing the aristocratic ghetto of Piccadilly. If its path is plotted, one can see that the delightfully named Shug Lane was just one of the doomed roads. The Hay Market (6/8) was also moved out to Regent's Park.

On the right of Rocque's map is Leicester Fields (5/9), not yet a square. On its north side is Leicester House and here, from 1736, the respective Princes of Wales customarily established a rival camp hostile to the Court. On the east side of Leicester Fields, at no.30, lived the painter and engraver William Hogarth

and his wife Jane from 1733. When surveying the fields, John Rocque would no doubt have seen Hogarth's sign of 'The Golden Head' hanging outside his door, a bust he had made of the artist van Dyck. Hogarth also had a country residence down in Chiswick, but Leicester Fields was his main home and it was here that he died in October 1764. For the last few years of his life another famous artist, Sir Joshua Reynolds, lived just opposite Hogarth at no.47.

The district above Leicester Fields was by Rocque's day going steadily downhill. The powerful had moved westwards, allowing the area to become an immigrants' quarter. A Greek colony had been based here in the seventeenth century, hence Greek Street, and in Rocque's time several hundred French Huguenots moved in. The historian John Strype in the 1720s remarked on 'the abundance of French people' in places like Old Compton Street (2/9). There were still elegant sites: from the 1770s the potter Josiah Wedgwood had his London base at nos.12-13 Greek Street:

We must have an elegant, extensive and Convenient showroom, for you know that my present sort of Customers will not mix with the rest of the world.

During the Victorian period, Soho was one of the most squalid parts of London, attracting hordes of political refugees, amongst them Karl Marx and his family who lived in Dean Street in the 1850s. Under the Metropolitan Board of Works' roadbuilding programme, Shaftesbury Avenue was pushed through many of the worst rookeries and slums in 1886, displacing some 3,000 people. The tower of Wren's St. Anne's (3/8), which is all that survives after German bombing, has since seen the district gain a reputation for its restaurants and for its sex-shops.

27

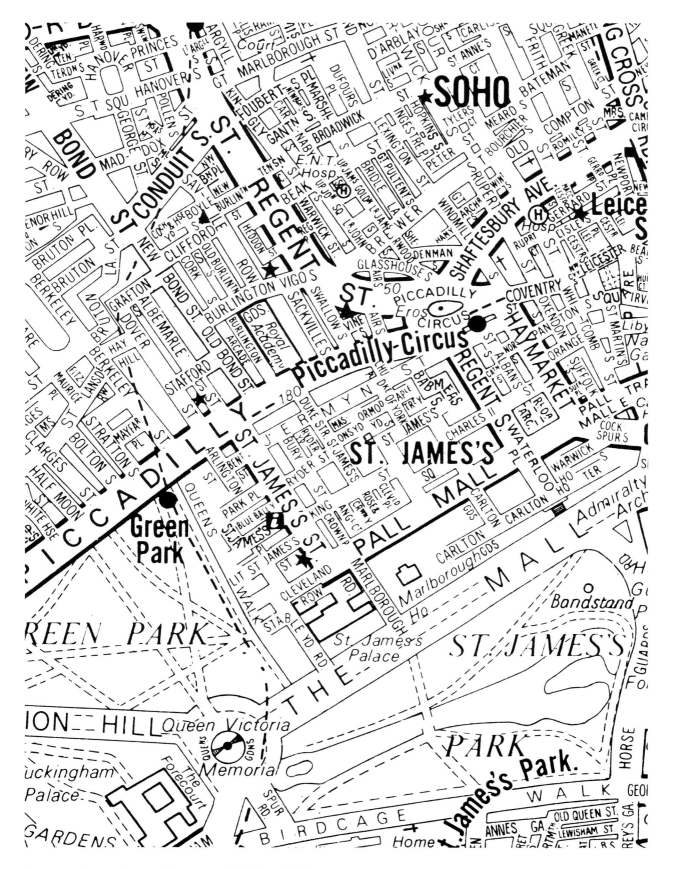

Reproduced by permission of Geographers' A-Z Map Co Ltd.

Westminster and Pimlico

Rocque's map shows what little there was of mid-eighteenth century London to the south of St. James's Park and to the west of the Houses of Parliament. Most of the area is taken up by Tothill Fields – a 'toot hill' was a beacon or observation point – with the Thames lying to the south. That Tothill Fields were often waterlogged indicates the problems facing many Londoners before the Thames was embanked in the second half of the nineteenth century.

Since the Middle Ages Tothill Fields had been used for a variety of purposes by the inhabitants of the capital, from bull-baiting and bear-gardens to duelling and convenient rubbish dump. A three-day fair was held outside Rochester Row (5/6). During the Civil War, Oliver Cromwell quartered 4,000 Royalist prisoners here, resulting in the death of over 1,200 of them from a fever contracted in the marshy fields: the survivors were sold off as slaves to the merchants of Guinea and Barbados. During the Plague of 1665, Tothill Fields served as a plague pit; Pepys noted in his *Diary* for July 18th 1665:

> I was much troubled this day to hear at Westminster how the officers do bury the dead in the open Tuttle Fields, pretending want of room elsewhere.

Perhaps it is just as well that, in view of these activities, hardly any of the Tothill Fields are with us today, other than the large Vincent Square which is the playing field of Westminster School. Ironically enough, the Royal Horticultural Halls are on the north side of Vincent Square.

The other major feature which takes up much of Rocque's map is the Chelsea Water Works (6/2) on the left. Opened in the early eighteenth century they were fed by the Thames, and as this river was also used as a sewage outlet it can be imagined that the water supplied to Westminster was not at all healthy. Fortunately its functions were usurped in the second half of the Victorian period by the Metropolitan Board of Works and the waterworks were consequently filled in and built over.

Several of the buildings surveyed by Rocque have survived the last 250 years. For example there are the almshouses (5/6) situated at the top of Tothill Fields; first erected by the Reverend James Palmer in 1656 for the benefit of 'Six Poor old Men and Six Poor old Women', they were extended by a Mr. Emery Hill in 1708. In 1881 the almshouses were rebuilt as the United Westminster almshouses, although busts of Palmer and Hill remain on the outside wall. The road which then and now runs past the front is called Rochester Row, confirming that much of this land had once been owned by the Bishops of Rochester.

To the right of the almshouses is the 'Gray Coat School' (4/7), still on the same site now even if most of the buildings are post-2nd World War. Here since 1701, the figures of a boy and girl in appropriate eighteenth-century costume are attached to the frontage. Today the Greatcoat Hospital is a day school for girls. Lady Dacre's Almshouses (2/5) had been established in 1600 for the purpose of 'bringing up children in virtue'; they were pulled down in the 1870s.

The Artillery Ground (3/7), in the 1740s a useful practice spot on the outskirts of London, has survived only in the names of Artillery Row and Artillery Mansions in Victoria Street. Stretton Grounds (3/8) has become Strutton Ground and holds a week-day market. Greencoat School (4/6), set up in 1633 for orphans, has left behind only Greencoat Place and Row. Joined onto it, Rocque shows the Bridewell (4/6) which, like its counterpart near Fleet Street, was a house of correction for women – for women, that is, paid for sexual services but not for those who did the paying. In Hogarth's *A Harlot's Progress* of 1731, Moll Hackabout is depicted here beating hemp and being threatened by the warders. This Bridewell remained in force until 1836.

Mention of the Bridewell is a reminder that parts of Westminster were very decrepit and poverty-stricken, particularly that district known as 'the Devil's Acre' which was centred on Orchard Street (2/9), Pye Street (3/9) and Peter Street (4/8). In their book on London published in 1872, Doré and Jerrold struggled to convey the former squalor of the area:

The Devil's Acre is, happily, almost a solitude now. The light of heaven has been admitted through the pestilent dens, the foul byeways, the kens and fences of wicked Westminster. Yet there are terrible highways and passages round about the Abbey still – as there are indeed about all the fairer parts of the metropolis.

Two methods adopted by the Victorians for clearing up slum areas were both tried here. The first involved the building of new churches: hence St. Stephen's, paid for by Angela Burdett Coutts, in Rochester Row from 1847, and the church of St. Matthew of 1850 in Great Peter Street. A few years later the Catholic Westminster Cathedral was built in the area. The second technique called for drastic roadbuilding schemes, and Victoria Street was opened in 1851, ploughing a way through some of Westminster's worst spots. Victoria Station itself was constructed in 1860.

Apart from Victoria Street this part of Rocque's map has been transformed by several other main roads. Rocque shows the 'Road to the Horse Ferry' (5/8), the only crossing over the Thames to Lambeth until Westminster Bridge was opened in 1750. In the 1740s the ferry charges were 2d for a man and a horse; 1/6 for a coach and two horses; and 2/6 for 'a Cart loaden'. Although Rocque indicates on the left the road which later became our Buckingham Palace Road, there is no sign of Vauxhall Bridge Road or Belgrave Road. Warwick Way was a tree-lined path (9/2).

Petty France (1/6) was so named because in the Middle Ages it had been occupied by French wool merchants, and it is worth remembering that London had several of these 'foreign' ghettoes in its midst: there were the Germans in Upper Thames Street, the Scots and Scotland Yard near Whitehall, a Petty Wales

beside the Tower of London and a Danish community near the church of St. Clement Danes.

The bulk of Rocque's map is now our Pimlico, then a village: in 1687 Pimlico was recorded as having a population of four people. However in the early nineteenth century it was developed by the builder Thomas Cubitt for the ground landlord, the Duke of Westminster. Cubitt headed a workforce of over 1,000 individuals, and, unlike his predecessor John Nash, had established a reputation for solid craftsmanship. His Pimlico project was on a less grand scale than that of neighbouring Belgravia, and for some years the inhabitants of Pimlico preferred to describe themselves as living in 'South Belgravia'. An alternative, more modern name is 'Stuccoville', conveying the smart, elegant but slightly monotonous style with which Cubitt carried out his work here. Naturally he ensured that open spaces were near at hand: Eccleston Square, Warwick Square, St. George's Gardens.

The 'Neat Houses' (13/9) at the bottom of Rocque's map would now be at the side of the noisy Grosvenor Road, the thoroughfare which runs around the northern rim of this part of the Thames. The name 'Grosvenor' derives from the French 'gros veneur' or great hunter, the name of William the Conqueror's nephew. According to James Dowsing the Grosvenor family claim to be descended from this Norman, but it was not until Sir Thomas Grosvenor married Mary Davies, heiress to the Manor of Ebury, in 1677 that his family began to leave their mark permanently on the map of London.

The contrast between the 1740s and the 1980s is telling: Rocque's Tothill Fields are uninhabited, whereas now for example Churchill Gardens Estate in Pimlico houses more than 5,000 people and Dolphin Square contains over 1,000 flats. The fact that the two maps do not provide a perfect fit points up Rocque's difficulties when surveying large open expanses.

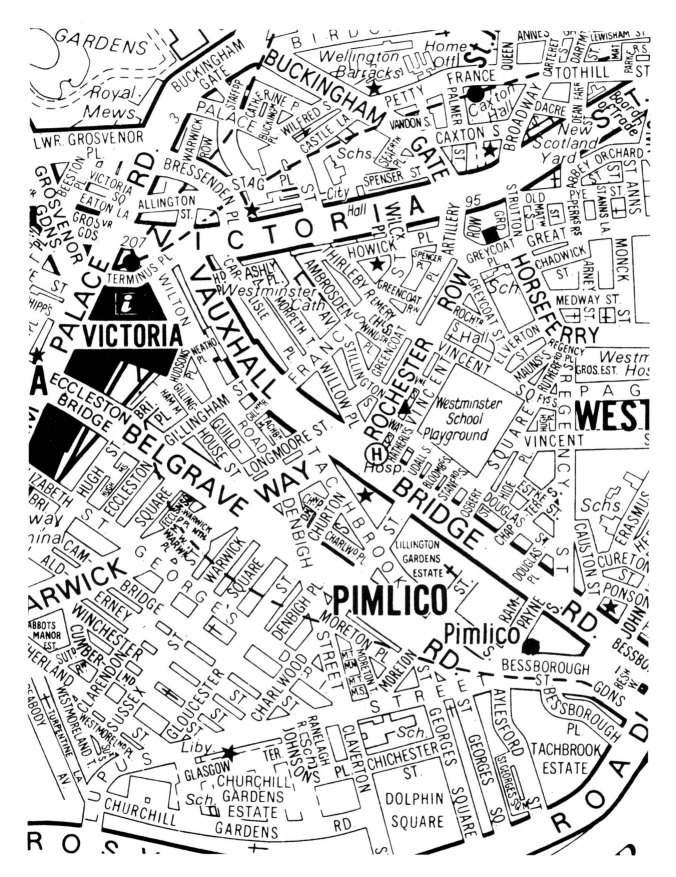

Reproduced by permission of Geographers' A-Z Map Co Ltd.

Bloomsbury and Holborn

Rocque's map emphasises yet again that in the middle of the eighteenth century there was no such place or area as 'North London'. One can see the Road to Hampstead and Highgate straggling up to the north; today it is our Gray's Inn Road. In this section the contrast is very marked between the undeveloped and open top half and the bottom half of the survey which does resemble modern London quite closely.

Lamb's Conduit Fields were so named because of the conduit or water channel introduced by a Mr. William Lamb in the sixteenth century in order to bring fresh water supplies to the capital. In the centre of the fields is the Foundling Hospital (4/6) started by the retired sea captain Thomas Coram. Horrified by the abandoned children which he saw dumped in the London streets, Coram campaigned for the establishment of some kind of charitable institution. Despite initial apathy, a Royal Charter was eventually granted in 1739 to 'The Hospital for the maintenance and education of exposed and deserted young children'. Three years later, the foundation stone was laid here on land specially bought at a cost of £7,000, and the doors were opened in 1745. Unfortunately the flood of mothers who descended on the hospital was so great that a balloting system for admission had to be instigated.

Amongst those public figures who helped the Foundling Hospital were Handel and William Hogarth who both became governors, as indeed did John Pine who engraved Rocque's map. In 1740 Hogarth painted a magnificent portrait of Coram and Handel sponsored annual charity performances of his *Messiah*; he also left the original score to the hospital in his will. The institution has since moved away from London but some of the original buildings survive and the children's playground now on the site is in the aptly named Coram's Fields.

At the back of the Foundling Hospital, Rocque shows the burial ground of St. George's, Bloomsbury. The church itself is some way off (11/13), indicating the eighteenth-century practice of separating the two, no doubt with memories of the plague of 1665 in mind.

The Foundling Hospital in the mid-eighteenth century, familiar to Hogarth, Handel and John Pine. The villages of Hampstead and Highgate are in the far distance.

The burial ground is now St. George's Gardens. On either side of Coram's Fields today are Brunswick Square and Mecklenburg Square, both names testifying to the royal family's German connections. Rocque's Black Mary's Hole (3/9) marks the beginning of our King's Cross Road.

The bottom half of Rocque's map is full of squares and open spaces which break up the already developed area. The largest of them is Lincoln's Inn Fields (12/8), often eyed up by builders with a nose for profit. In the previous century only a desperate rearguard action led by the pupils at the adjacent Inn of Court had kept off the builders, and in 1635 Inigo Jones laid out the fields in a more formal fashion. In 1735 they were railed around the outside in order to discourage their use by beggars and prostitutes. On the south side Rocque shows Lincoln's Inn Theatre, built in 1661 and the venue for the first pantomime staged in this country in 1716. In January 1728 John Gay's enormously successful play *The Beggar's Opera* was produced, a triumph which paradoxically finished this theatre: its proprietor John Rich was sufficiently encouraged to open another playhouse at Covent Garden and the one here closed in the late 1730s. Its site is now occupied by the Royal College of Surgeons.

Of the three other squares surveyed by John Rocque, Bloomsbury Square (10/4) gave its name to the area. Red Lion Square (9/6) was associated with duels and like Lincoln's Inn Fields was nearly developed by builders. Connected both with this square and also the Foundling Hospital was Jonas Hanway, the man credited with introducing the umbrella to this country. Today Hanway House stands on the site of the dwelling on the north side where he had lived and died in 1786.

In Rocque's day Queen's Square (4/7) had only just been laid out, named after the late Queen Anne when the artist and writer William Morris lived here in 1865, he was still able to view the Hampstead heights from an upstairs window.

Russell Square to the north of Bedford House (9/4) was still unfinished by the 1740s, but although Bedford House has not survived, Montagu House (10/2) on its west side has, albeit under the name of the British Museum and substantially rebuilt. Financed by means of a public lottery, the statute introducing the British Museum was passed in 1753. The bulk of the collection came from the libraries of two individuals mentioned elsewhere in this book: Sir Hans Sloane and Robert Harley, the 1st Earl of Oxford.

No more than a few hundred yards away from Montague and Bedford Houses, Rocque shows the tiny village of St. Giles (13/1), its poverty and squalor providing a striking contrast to the aristocratic splendour just up the road. The church of St. Giles was on the site of a former leper colony but it had been rebuilt as recently as 1734 by a Mr. Henry Flitcroft – hence our Flitcroft Street to the side of the church. Henry Fielding's infant son James was buried here in 1734. The church was famous for its 'St. Giles Bowl', offered to the condemned travelling westward to Tyburn. No doubt the potent alcoholic brew helped to dull the senses.

The church was ringed by rookeries and dirty alleys; the historian Dorothy George has written that of the 2,000 houses in eighteenth-century St. Giles over 500 were gin-shops and another 82 were 'twopenny houses' and brothels[7]. Hogarth's engraving *Gin Lane* of 1751 was set in the neighbourhood, and he shows a notice over a doorway which reads 'Drunk for a penny; dead drunk for two-pence; clean straw for nothing'.

In the background of *Gin Lane* can be seen a church surmounted by a statue: the church was St. George's, Bloomsbury (11/3) and the statue was of George I. Both remain today. The wealthy had been attracted to this area in the early eighteenth century by the then healthy air of Holborn, and they of course desired their own church. It was provided for them by Nicholas

Hawksmoor in 1731 under the 50 New Churches Act; although having to squeeze it between already existing buildings the architect managed to give it a splendid portico, one of the first in London. Inside the church the Duke of Bedford and his family had reserved for their private use the whole of the South gallery, the Duke of Montague and his family the North gallery. David Garrick was married here in 1749. Bloomsbury Market (11/4) was never successful and died in the 1780s.

Among the changes here since Rocque's time – quite apart from the disappearance of Lamb's Conduit Fields – New Oxford Street was constructed in the 1840s to clear away some of the slums. It joined up with the widened Theobalds Road and Liquorpond Road (7/10) became Clerkenwell Road. Kingsway opened in 1905 was another slum clearance project.

Lincoln's Inn still retains much of the charm and unhurried atmosphere which Rocque must have encountered whilst carrying out his survey. The Gate House (12/10) into Chancery Lane dated back to 1517 and remains today although rebuilt during the 1960s, whilst the Chapel of 1619-23 was probably by Inigo Jones. Another Inn of Court, Gray's Inn (9/10), also boasted gracious surroundings. Of the famous individuals who have been entered at both establishments, the one who put his name down at Lincoln's Inn in 1737, the year that Rocque began his work, never became a barrister: instead David Garrick went off to found a wine business with his brother before going on the stage.

Hogarth's *Gin Lane* of 1751; Hawksmoor's church of St. George's, Bloomsbury is shown in the background.

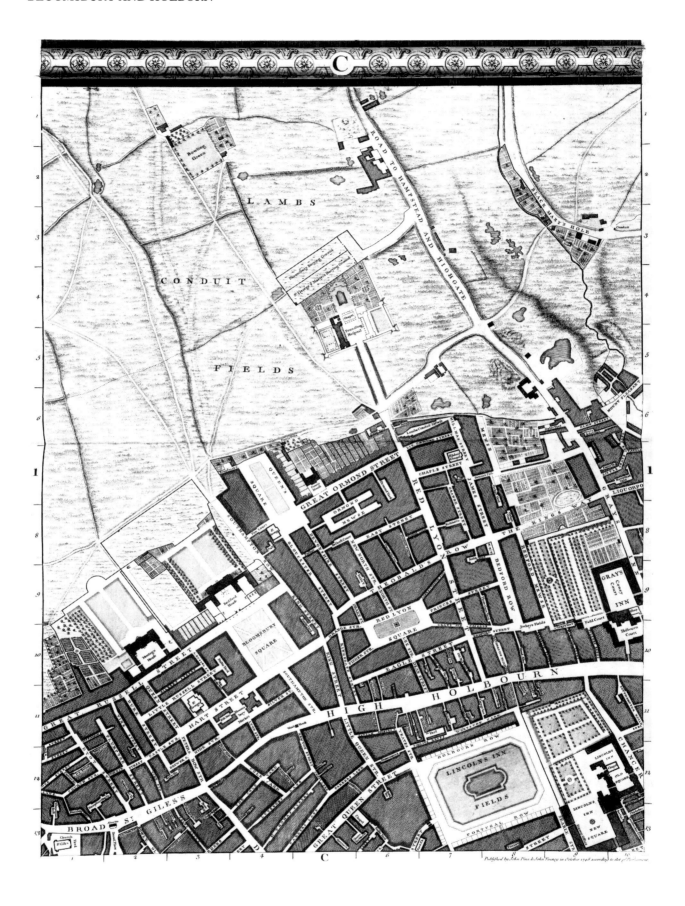

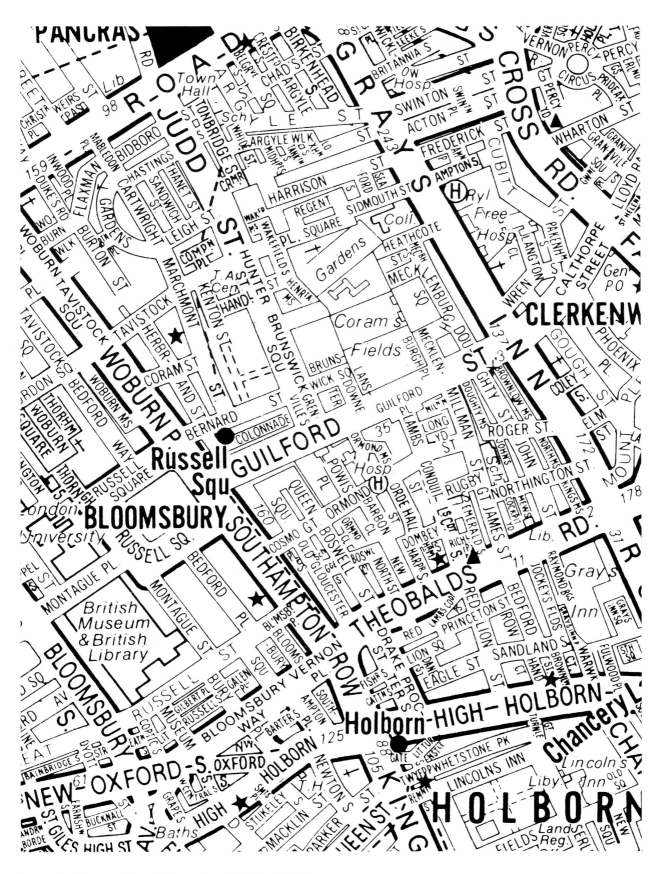

Covent Garden, Whitehall and Lambeth

The glaring contrast in this portion of Rocque's London is yet again between the built-up north side of the river where many of our modern streets and roads can be quickly identified, and the south side which is barely inhabited. Apart from timber yards and wharves there is little other than Cuper's Garden (9/9), a pleasure resort with a somewhat unsavoury reputation which eventually closed down in 1760, and a bowling green.

However the south's openness was soon to change and Rocque shows the agent behind this transformation, although it did not in fact open for some four years after Rocque's map was published in 1746: Westminster Bridge. Only the second bridge across the Thames, the very notion of such a crossing had been opposed by the City of London, who feared that it would draw away trade from their own London Bridge, and also by the watermen. Built by the Swiss engineer Charles Labelye it was at one point the target of attempted sabotage; according to Sir John Summerson, a pier subsided and the bridge's completion was delayed for several years. The cost of nearly £400,000 was raised in part from a state run lottery, leading Henry Fielding to christen it 'the bridge of fools'. Once it opened, the other side of the river became much more accessible and therefore favoured by trade and commerce. Waterloo Station of 1848 covers much of this site and to the north is now the South Bank complex of National Theatre, National Film Theatre and Festival Hall, appropriately enough where Cuper's Garden once stood.

Why was the north side of the Thames as shown here so developed by the 1740s? In the Middle Ages the City and Westminster – or the two poles of finance and royal power – had been joined by the Strand. Along this major thoroughfare several nobles had placed their mansions, amongst them being the Savoy Palace which has given its name to a hotel and a theatre. Later the Duke of Somerset built his Somerset House here (4/7) in the middle of the sixteenth century. Oliver Cromwell's body had been laid in Somerset House after his death in 1658, his unpopularity prompting the crowd to throw muck and rubbish at the outside of the building. In Rocque's day it saw the first meeting of the Guardians of the Foundling Hospital in November 1739. By then the area around the Strand had been filled in with buildings.

The first landowner to have started this process had been the 4th Earl of Bedford who owned the estates or 'convent garden' once tended by the monks of Westminster Abbey. He employed the architect Inigo Jones to design a piazza and also, in 1633, the church of St. Paul's (4/4). The portico of this church had served many purposes, from the first puppet shows in England to a convenient meeting-place for prostitutes. Throughout Rocque's time it hosted the hustings for the Westminster elections, violent affairs which were spread out over two weeks. Heads were broken and blood spilt, with one eighteenth-century observer expressing his revulsion towards

a scene only ridiculous and disgusting. The vulgar abuse of the candidates from the vilest rabble is not rendered endurable by either wit or good temper.

From 1671 the famous market was held here, an activity which caused the fashionable to abandon the neighbourhood, starting with the Duke of Bedford himself in the early eighteenth century. The area soon became known for its brothels and gaming-houses often depicted by Hogarth, and the local magistrate Sir John Fielding observed of Covent Garden that

One would imagine that all the prostitutes in the kingdom had picked up on that blessed neighbourhood, for here are lewd women enough to fill a mighty colony.

Sir John's elder half-brother, Henry, had lived on the west side of Bow Street (3/5) from December 1748 when he was appointed magistrate for Westminster, writing there his novel *Tom Jones* and also founding the Bow Street Runners in 1749, from which emerged the modern police force.

Also shown on Rocque's map – although not very clearly – are the two patent theatres of Covent Garden (3/4) and Drury Lane (3/6). Both were plagued by unruly audiences and when in 1743 David Garrick was performing at Drury Lane, 30 prize-fighters had to be sent in to quell the riots occurring in the auditorium. Two years before, the same theatre had witnessed the first production of the *Messiah*, conducted in person by the composer Handel.

This section of Rocque's survey depicted a number of other squalid areas, such as Seven Dials (2/2) which was rapidly deteriorating in terms of prestige, and the area around Clare Market (1/7), later demolished in order to make way for Kingsway. There was also the aptly named Thieving Lane (14/1) in Westminster near the Houses of Parliament, a legacy of the days when Westminster Abbey had offered a place of sanctuary for wrongdoers. The Victorian development of Parliament Square and Victoria Street transformed this neighbourhood.

Other changes since Rocque's day include the Victoria Embankment. Before its introduction the Thames was much broader, more stagnant and consequently more smelly than today. In 1858, dubbed the year of 'The Great Stink', the odours from the river were such that MPs in the House of Commons had to speak with a handkerchief clapped firmly to their noses. The Embankment narrowed the river's passage as well as wiping out the many stairs visible on Rocque's map.

Another major development since the 1740s has been the creation of Trafalgar Square. Before this change Charing Cross (8/2) was a bottleneck, the flow of traffic being impeded by the statue of Charles I on his horse which stood at the top of Whitehall. It was also where the pillory was sited: in July 1703 when Daniel Defoe was placed here, he found himself garlanded with flowers by the crowds rather than trying to dodge bricks. Rocque's Royal Mews (7/1) had catered for hawks and then horses, but in the 1820s William Wilkins built the National Gallery here. Trafalgar Square was officially opened in 1830. Northumberland House (7/2) was pulled down and replaced by Northumberland Avenue in the mid-1870s. Shaftesbury Avenue and Charing Cross Road tidied up the top left-hand corner and Hungerford Market (7/3) fell victim to Charing Cross Station.

Several of the buildings surveyed by John Rocque have in fact survived the last 250 years. The medieval Whitehall Palace had given its name to the surroundings, and although largely destroyed by the 1740s, its jousting ground became the Horse Guards' Parade (10/1). Downing Street (11/2) of course remains, and no. 10 was established as the residence of the 1st Lord of the Treasury or Prime Minister. Sir Robert Walpole had been the first such to occupy it, from 1735 to 1742. Incidentally the man who gave his name to the street, Sir George Downing, had once been Pepys' boss; the latter observed in his *Diary* that 'He is so stingy a fellow I care not to see him.'

St. Martin-in-the-Fields (6/2) had once, as its name suggests, stood in the countryside, but not in the 1720s when it was rebuilt by James Gibbs. Further along the Strand were and are St. Mary-le-Strand (3/7), another of the 50 New Churches, and St. Clement Danes (2/9), both of which stand among hurtling traffic. The name of the latter is evidence of the Danish colony which had been here from the days of Alfred the Great. The importance of the Strand as a busy highway had been recognised by a Captain Bailey, a retired sea-captain, who set up the first hackney-coach stand by St. Clement Danes in 1634, the forerunner of our taxicab service.

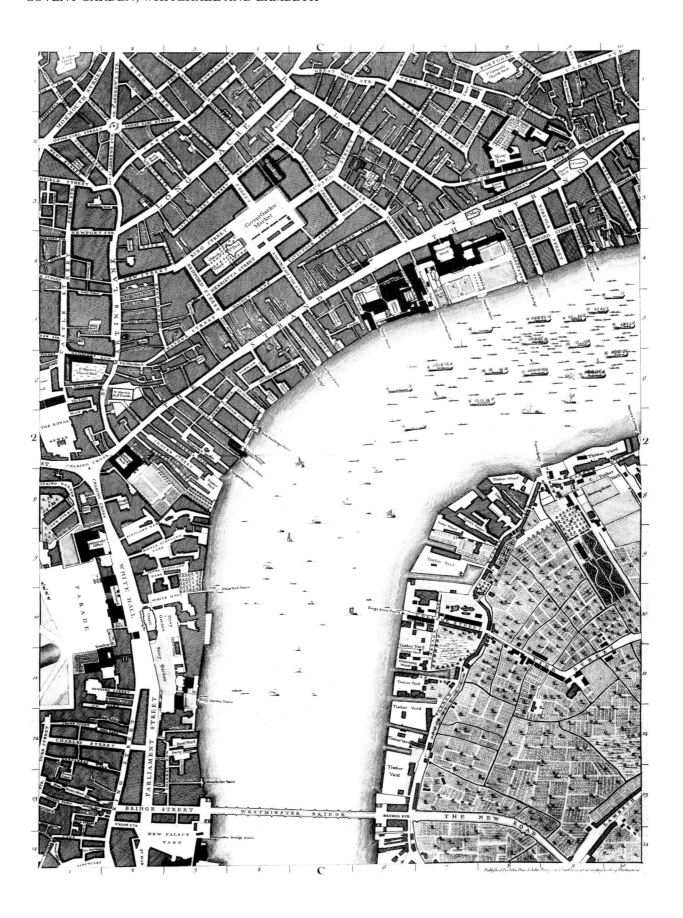

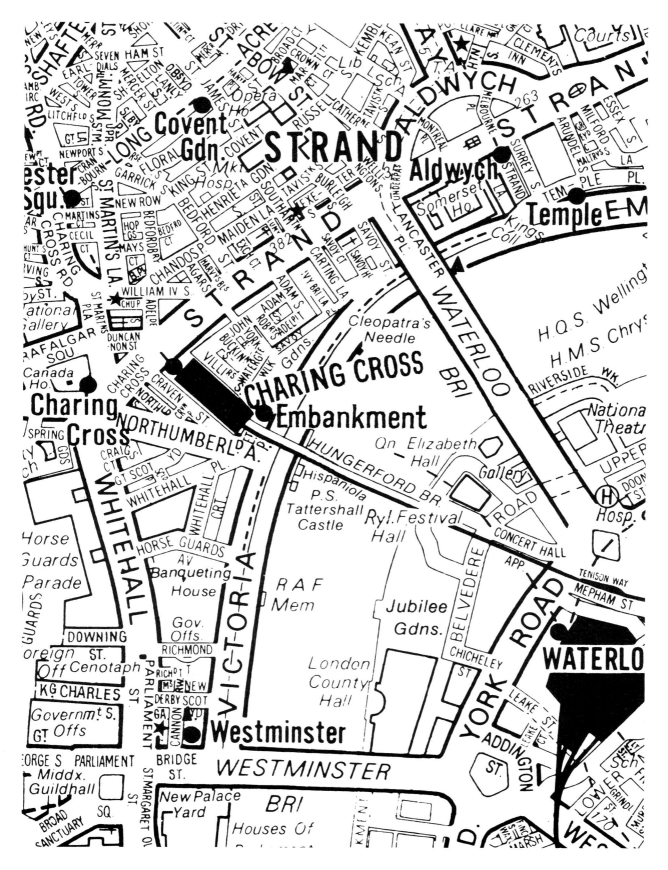

Reproduced by permission of Geographers' A-Z Map Co Ltd.

Westminster and Vauxhall

The differences here on Rocque's map are between Westminster and Vauxhall in the 1740s and also between Vauxhall now and 250 years ago. The explanation for Lambeth and Vauxhall's slow development was that not only did the unembanked Thames often overflow into the streets and houses on the south bank, but the area anyway was damp and unhealthy. In Tudor times the marshes of Lambeth were much used for concealing the corpses of unwanted children or other inconvenient individuals.

Communication between the two sides of the Thames was not easy: apart from the Thames watermen depicted by Rocque – who often used six- or even eight-oar wherries and were in any case famed for their foul language – there was only the horse ferry. The landing spots are shown (5/3 and 6/5). Not that this was an infallible method of crossing, as Oliver Cromwell found out once when his coach sank unceremoniously in midstream. Today Lambeth Bridge, opened in 1862, guarantees a safer passage.

On the Lambeth side of the Thames Rocque shows Lambeth Palace (5/5), then and now the home of the Archbishop of Canterbury. Its twelfth-century origins lay in the wish of successive Archbishops to escape from the watchful eyes of the monks based at Canterbury Cathedral. Lambeth was far enough away to meet this purpose but just as significantly it was close to the kings' power base at Westminster and Whitehall. In Rocque's time Lambeth Palace was still recovering from the privations of the Civil War when a regiment of troops and their horses had been garrisoned here: the chapel had been used as a dancing-room. Archbishop Juxon's Great Hall of the late seventeenth century survives today.

Just to the south of the Palace is St. Mary's (5/6), the parish church of Lambeth. Its tower which would have been known to Rocque was virtually the only part of the old church which survived the Victorian rebuilding of 1851. The church is now a museum of gardening history, primarily because the Tradescants father and son, famed in the seventeenth century for their collecting of flowers and trees, were both buried here;

as indeed in 1817 was the Captain Bligh of 'Mutiny on the Bounty' renown.

The only other major activity on this side of the Thames in the Georgian period took place further south: Vauxhall Gardens (13/6). Not as exclusive but more popular than the Ranelagh Gardens, Vauxhall was noted for its music and fancy-dress balls. Between 1728 and 1767 the Gardens were run by Jonathan Tyers, hence today's Jonathan and Tyers Streets. In 1732 the young William Hogarth had summer lodgings in the vicinity, with the result that he and Tyers became close friends; over the years Hogarth designed several pass-tickets for Vauxhall Gardens and allowed copies of his paintings to be exhibited free of charge. Tyers also commissioned the sculptor Roubiliac to produce a statue of the composer Handel and this stood in the middle of the Gardens from 1738.

Reactions to Vauxhall Gardens differed, as Tobias Smollett showed in his novel *Humphry Clinker*; the niece found the place

crowded with the gayest company, ranging through those blissful shades, or supping in different lodges on cold collations, enlivened with mirth, freedom, and good-humour, and animated by an excellent band of music.

The uncle by contrast considered that

the walks which Nature seems to have intended for solitude, shade, and silence, are filled with crowds of noisy people, sucking up the nocturnal rheums of an agueish climate; and through these gay scenes a few lamps glimmer like so many penny farthing candles.

Despite Tyers' best efforts, an aura of immorality clung to the Vauxhall Gardens because of their abundant 'dark walks' and in 1764 they were temporarily closed. But they reopened and had the last laugh, outliving all of London's other pleasure gardens and not shutting down until 1859.

The 'Plate Glass House' (12/5) above the Gardens has left behind only the present Glasshouse Walk, but this is more than the little boat-builders' yards which were swept away completely when the Albert Embankment was built in the 1860s.

A 1754 view of Vauxhall Gardens which shows the 'dark walks' used by lovers.

Looking at the Westminster side of the river, several landmarks familiar today also show up in Rocque's map. Most obvious is Westminster or St. Peter's Abbey (1/1), built by Edward the Confessor as compensation for not embarking on a pilgrimage to the Holy Land. James Boswell called it 'this magnificent and venerable temple' in 1763 and does not seem to have objected to the poor of the parish who were allowed to beg in the aisles even when services were being conducted. Above the Abbey lies St. Margaret's (1/2), the parish church of the House of Commons. Both Samuel Pepys and John Milton had been married here. Still further north one can glimpse Westminster Hall and the old Houses of Parliament (1/3). In 1738, at the time of Rocque's survey, the House of Lords decided to ban women from witnessing their debates, whereupon a determined group of them began smashing and kicking at the locked door 'with so much violence, that the speakers in the house were scarce heard'. The women then changed their tactics, keeping deadly quiet for half an hour; sure enough

the Chancellor, who thought this a certain proof of their absence . . . gave orders for the opening of the door; upon which they all rushed in, pushed aside their competitors, and placed themselves in the front row of the gallery.

Another survivor since Rocque's day is Westminster School (2/1), once attached to the Abbey but then refounded by Elizabeth I. Sir Christopher Wren had been a pupil here, together with John Cleland the author of *Memoirs of a Woman of Pleasure*, also known as *Fanny Hill*. Further south is St. John's Yard, now Smith Square, with the church of St. John sitting in the middle. This was the most expensive of all the churches completed under the 50 New Churches Act. Its four towers were designed to provide an even weight in the

soft ground. It is now a concert hall. St. John's burial ground was a little way off (5/1) and today, as St. John's Gardens, is sandwiched between two rather grim blocks of the Westminster Hospital. Founded in 1716 this hospital had been the first to be supported wholly through voluntary contributions from the public.

On the edge of the riverside can be seen numerous wharves, indicating yet again the Thames's important role in eighteenth-century life. The Millbank – there had been a mill used by the Abbey in the Middle Ages – can be seen heading south. Nicholas Hawksmoor, architect of many Georgian churches as well as the assistant to Wren on St. Paul's and surveyor-general of Westminster Abbey, had died at his home here in March 1736. Apparently Hawksmoor was noted for his good temper despite the fact that he suffered 'the most poignant pains of the gout'. Today Millbank is very much wider than in the 1740s and the Victoria Tower Gardens have wiped out the wharves.

The road stops abruptly at Grosvenor House (5/3), one of the town residences of the Grosvenor family, otherwise the Dukes of Westminster. The 2nd Marquess of Westminster, the man largely responsible for the development of Belgravia and Pimlico, was born in this house in 1795. The gardens of Grosvenor House are now occupied by the Queen Alexandra Military Hospital.

In Rocque's day there were only open fields to the south, but in 1816 the Millbank penitentiary was built. Called a 'model prison' it housed convicts waiting to be transported to Australia. In 1892 the prison was pulled down: the Tate Gallery now stands on the site. Vauxhall Bridge was opened in 1816.

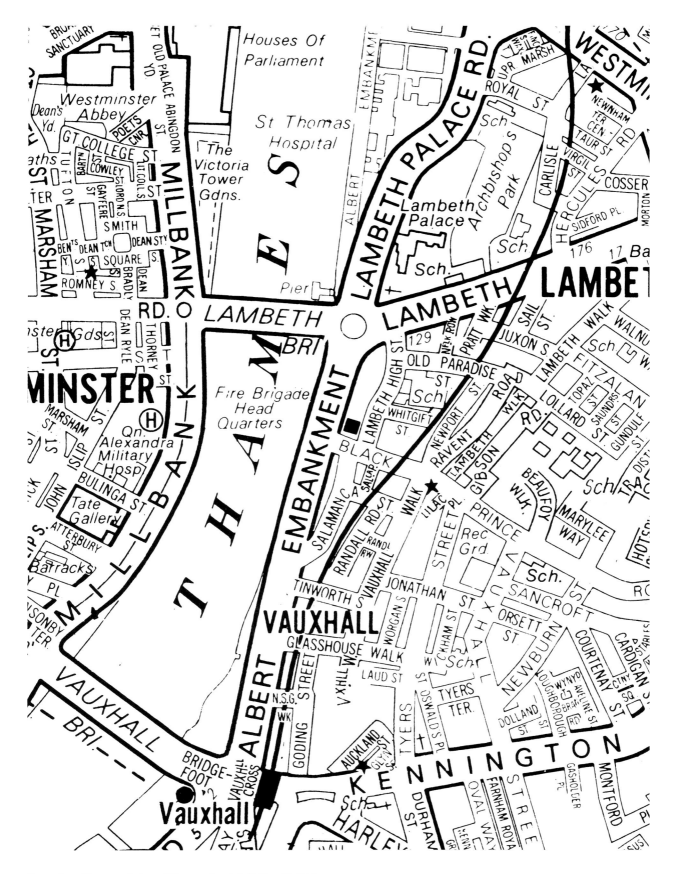

Clerkenwell and Smithfield

In the Middle Ages both Clerkenwell and Smithfield were largely open fields. However during the seventeenth century the area began to be built over, a process accelerated by the Great Fire of 1666: many City dwellers fled here and camped out in tents, but not all of them returned after the fire had died out. Several nobles such as the Duke of Newcastle owned fine mansions around Clerkenwell Green (6/5), although by the time of Rocque's survey they were moving westwards towards Mayfair and Cavendish Square, their places being taken by a multitude of skilled craftsmen such as engravers, jewellers, printers and silversmiths.

There were a number of reasons why Clerkenwell and Smithfield proved unable to retain the fashionable, all of them clearly displayed on Rocque's map. First of all there was Smithfield Market (10/6) which entailed the herding of livestock through the narrow streets nearby, causing dirt, noise and confusion. On the same spot every year in August Bartholomew Fair was also held, a jamboree which by the 1740s offered revellers the opportunity to let off steam in convivial but rowdy company.

Just beside the actual gate of Newgate (12/6) lay the notorious Newgate prison, the biggest and worst of all the London gaols. Daniel Defoe had been incarcerated here only a few years before Rocque began his survey and in his novel *Moll Flanders* of 1722 has left us a graphic description of the prison as it appeared to Moll:

> 'tis impossible to describe the terror of my mind, when I was first brought in, and when I looked round upon all the horrors of that dismal place I looked on myself as lost, and that I had nothing to think of but of going out of the world, and that with the utmost infamy: the hellish noise, the roaring, swearing, and clamour, the stench and nastiness, and all the dreadful crowd of afflicting things that I saw there, joined together to make the place seem an emblem of hell itself, and a kind of entrance into it.

Many inmates died of gaol fever and not until 1770 was Newgate prison rebuilt on a less cramped scale. It was from here that the condemned began the cart-ride to Tyburn – the origin of someone 'going west' – with the bells of St. Sepulchre's (12/6) sending them on their way. After 1783, executions took place in the road outside, and in public until 1868. There was a court attached to the prison and Henry Fielding in his *Tom Jones* refers to 'Newgate solicitors' who could be bribed to swear to anything. Newgate prison was finally demolished in the early years of this century and its site is now occupied by the Old Bailey.

A final drawback to living in this area was the existence of the Fleet River which flowed down from the north, its line roughly marked by our Farringdon Road and Street. In 1710 the *Tatler* had described the state of the river:

> Sweepings from butchers' stalls, dung, guts, and blood
> Drown'd puppies, shaking sprats, all drenched in mud,
> Dead cats, and turnip tops, come tumbling down the flood.

By 1733 most of the Fleet River had been covered over, a process finished off in 1766, but this did not by itself remove the rookeries and brothels which had grown up around the river: amongst them were Saffron Hill (9/4), the setting of parts of *Oliver Twist*, Turnmill Street (8/5), Chick Lane (10/5) and Cock Lane (11/6). Together they were sometimes called 'Jack Ketch's Warren', Jack Ketch being the traditional name given to the public hangman. These squalid neighbourhoods remained until the construction of Farringdon Road in the 1860s.

Several important features of Rocque's map can be seen today. St. John Street for example, which runs down the middle of the survey (7/6), was comparatively wide because of its use by drovers bringing their cattle to Smithfield. Clerkenwell Green (6/5) retains the same dimensions and Charterhouse (7/7) – once a priory whose initiates had included the young Thomas More, but in the 1740s a school and now a part of Barts Hospital – has kept several of its old buildings.

Barts Hospital itself is on the south side of West

Thomas Coram (1668-1751) the retired sea captain who set up the Foundling Hospital: this portrait was painted by his friend and fellow governor William Hogarth.

survived both German bombing and modern redevelopment, amongst them being St. Andrew's by Holborn Hill (11/4). It now contains the tomb of Thomas Coram, the founder of the Founding Hospital, and also the pulpit, font and organ from its chapel. St. James (6/4) remains beside Clerkenwell Green, St. Sepulchre's on Newgate Street (12/6), and St. Ann's (12/9) and St. Botolph's Aldersgate (11/9) are still with us; near the latter, John Wesley experienced his conversion in May 1738. Of Wren's Christ Church (13/8) only the tower remains.

Hatton Garden (9/3) was in Rocque's day establishing a reputation for its jewellery and St. Etheldreda's (10/3) – Rocque shows only the chapel – is once again a Catholic church. Formerly the home of the Bishops of Ely, the chapel and crypt date back to the thirteenth century. St. John's Gate (7/6), which although straddling a road was not one of the seven City gates, had belonged to the Order of St. John of Jerusalem until their disbandment by Henry VIII. The church became the parish church of Clerkenwell and the Gate, built in 1504, housed a variety of enterprises – in fact in this small area many of the luminaries of Rocque's day gathered. The coffee house had been run by Richard Hogarth, William's father, and the Gate harboured the literary periodical *The Gentleman's Magazine* whose contributors included both Samuel Johnson and Oliver Goldsmith who often visited the offices. At the time of Rocque's survey the unknown David Garrick gave private theatrical performances here. Other literary associations were to be found in Little Britain (11/8) whose booksellers had often been patronised by Pepys.

The major developments since the 1740s have included Clerkenwell Road and also Holborn Viaduct, constructed in the 1860s in order to allow traffic to bypass the steep Holborn Hill.

But if the bottom third of Rocque's map is already heavily developed, the top section is another reminder of London's eighteenth-century limits. The New River (1/3) brought fresh water to London and is now the headquarters of the Thames Water Authority. The pleasure garden and theatre of Sadler's Wells lie just off the top of Rocque's map. Otherwise the fields here were notorious as a haunt of highwaymen waiting for travellers approaching London. In order to minimise this threat, coaching inns such as the Angel sprang up in Islington where groups of people could gather in numbers before crossing the fields.

Smithfield (11/7), exactly the same site which it has occupied ever since it was founded in the early twelfth century. Its own church of St. Bartholomew the Less, in which Inigo Jones was christened, is just visible in the hospital grounds. On the east side of West Smithfield is 'Great St. Bartholomew', established at the same time as the hospital and also by the ex-court jester turned monk Rahere. Today it is the oldest parish church in London – the Great Fire had petered out at Pye Corner (11/7). William Hogarth had been born in Bartholomew Close (8/10), and in later years he was a benefactor of Barts Hospital.

Several other churches shown by Rocque have

Reproduced by permission of Geographers' A-Z Map Co Ltd.

Fleet Street, St. Paul's and Southwark

Rocque's map offers a sharp contrast between the two banks of the Thames, the north side being dominated by landmarks familiar to us today such as Fleet Street and Wren's St. Paul's, whereas on the south, modern London is far less identifiable. The reason behind this differing pace of development is that, although Southwark had provided much of the capital's entertainment in the sixteenth and seventeenth centuries – it lay conveniently outside the boundary of the City – few people actually lived there. Instead, revellers were rowed to and fro across the Thames by the ubiquitous watermen; thus the number of stairs shown on both banks.

Some of the Southwark resorts can still be seen in Rocque's map, including Pye Garden (8/8) and, faintly, the Old Bear Gardens (8/10). The playhouses were further east. However during the Civil War the strength of the Puritan faction in London ensured that much more stringent regulations were enforced and many of Southwark's attractions closed down, failing to reopen after the Restoration in 1660.

Of this south side few buildings or institutions are with us today. One that has survived is Christ Church (9/4), the second church of this name: the first of 1670 had been built on insecure foundations and slowly sank into the mud. Rocque's building was completed in 1730 but destroyed by German bombing. Not far from Christ Church, Rocque shows Hopton's Almshouses (8/6), recently erected for '26 decayed housekeepers' through the munificence of a fishmonger called Charles Hopton. The chapel remains at the end of the buildings which at the present time are being refurbished. Otherwise this area in the 1740s was full of the tenter grounds used for stretching cloth and also marked by roads with evocative names: Melancholy Walk, Bandy Leg Walk, Dirty Lane. To the east are the beginnings of the built-up Southwark proper. Mint Street (12/10) was a criminal quarter, and one of the crooks in John Gay's *The Beggar's Opera* of 1728 is referred to as 'Matt of the Mint'. Today this part of Southwark is dominated by busy roads like Blackfriars Road; one can just about discover the paths in Rocque's survey

which later became The Cut and Union Street. Blackfriars Bridge itself was built in the 1760s, the third such crossing over the Thames, and financed in part from the fines levied on those not accepting the onerous post of Sheriff.

Rocque's map of the other side of the river emphasises the sheer size of Sir Christopher Wren's St. Paul's. Before the construction of skyscrapers and office blocks the cross which was 365ft. above ground level would have dominated the horizon – and in any case the cathedral stood on a hill. The building before Wren's had been used as a meeting-place by lawyers and prostitutes as well as a shortcut for anyone too lazy to walk around the outside. During the Civil War of the 1640s the church was turned into a stables and the valuable plate sold off in order to pay for the army's Irish campaigns. It was destroyed in the Great Fire, 1666. Wren began work on the new cathedral nine years later and finished in 1708; it had cost over £700,000. Defoe called it

a building exceeding beautiful and magnificent . . . no man that has the least judgment in building, that knows any thing of the rules of proportion, and will judge impartially, can find any fault in this church.

Boswell climbed to the very top in July 1763, losing his nerve halfway up the stairs but managing to complete the climb and finding the view of the hills of Hampstead and Highgate well worth the effort.

Of the other places near St. Paul's, Newgate Market (1/7) was already losing out to its rival of Smithfield. Pater Noster Row (1/8) was becoming by the 1740s a centre for publishing – *Robinson Crusoe* by Defoe had been first issued here in 1719. St. Martin's (1/6) remains on Ludgate Hill even though the Ludgate itself was soon to be demolished. To the south of the cathedral St. Andrew by the Wardrobe (3/7) remains, its unusual name deriving from the fact that after 1361 the Royal wardrobe had been situated in the neighbourhood. St. Benet's (4/8) and St. Nicholas Cole Abbey (3/9) have survived, but only the tower of St. Mary Somerset (4/9).

Hogarth's *Southwark Fair* of 1773 emphasises the turbulence of the proceedings which brought Southwark and thus the approach to London Bridge to a standstill.

Running down from the top of the map is the Fleet River, and one can clearly see that by the 1740s it had been covered over down to Fleet Bridge but from that point onwards remained an open sewer. On either side of the Fleet, Rocque depicts two notorious prisons. The first was the Fleet prison (1/5), considered preferable to Newgate but still without the segregation of the inmates and with a 'Begging Grate' out on the street offering many prisoners the only chance of their being fed, imploring passers-by to hand them scraps of food. It also functioned as a debtors' prison and William Hogarth's father Richard endured several spells here. The seventh plate of *The Rake's Progress* portrays Tom in this gaol. Another inmate was to be John Cleland who in 1748-49 took the opportunity to write and publish the erotic classic *Memoirs of a Woman of Pleasure*, also known as *Fanny Hill*. The prison was finally destroyed in 1846 and its only legacy is the name of Fleet Lane. The other prison was Bridewell (2/4), catering for women gaoled for sexual offences. It was a popular pastime to come and see the women whipped in public.

To the north of Bridewell lies St. Bridget's or St. Bride's (2/4) which suitably enough is the parish church of the press: Wynkyn de Worde, pupil of William Caxton, had moved his printing press nearby in 1550. Samuel Pepys had been born in Salisbury Court (2/4) in February 1633, and at the time of John Rocque's survey, Samuel Richardson lived here and was writing his novel *Pamela*, published in 1740. Until recently this whole area had been tainted by the existence of a sanctuary or criminal ghetto called Alsatia; troops cleared it in 1697.

By looking along to the west one sees the two Inns of Court called the Inner Temple and the Middle Temple on land once owned by the Knights Templars. This order had fallen foul of the kings who distrusted their secular powers. The area was leased off to the lawyers who have been here ever since; the round Temple church of 1185 (2/1) has remained partially intact. Oliver Goldsmith was buried to the north of the church in 1774.

On the north side of Fleet Street Rocque shows the church of St. Dunstan's in the West (1/2) which today stands further to the north after being rebuilt in 1831 to allow for the widening of Fleet Street. Still outside today is the statue of Elizabeth I which dates back to 1586 – the oldest statue in London – and which had once been on Ludgate. To the east of St. Dunstan's, Rocque puts in the maze of little alleys and streets, one of which contained the Cheshire Cheese public house. Another of these hideaways was Gough Square: Samuel Johnson occupied no.17 between 1746 and 1759, paying a rent of £30 per annum. His wife Tettie died here whilst he was at work on his famous *Dictionary*.

Temple Bar (2/1) had been rebuilt by Wren in the 1670s and its spikes sometimes held the heads of executed traitors. One shameless entrepreneur hired out eyeglasses so that spectators could obtain a better view. In 1878 Temple Bar was removed as constituting a traffic hazard and now sits in Theobald's Park.

The major change since Rocque's survey has been that masterpiece of Victorian engineering, the Embankment. If one compares the two maps, it is clear that the Thames in the 1740s was much wider than it is now. The Embankment was constructed on land reclaimed from the Thames and diminished significantly the importance of that river as a highway.

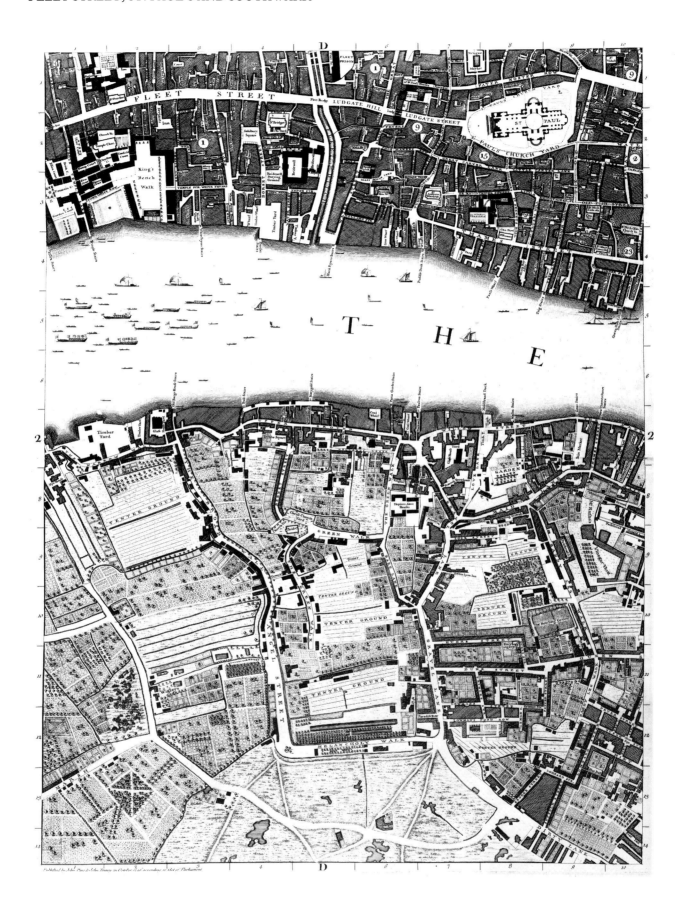

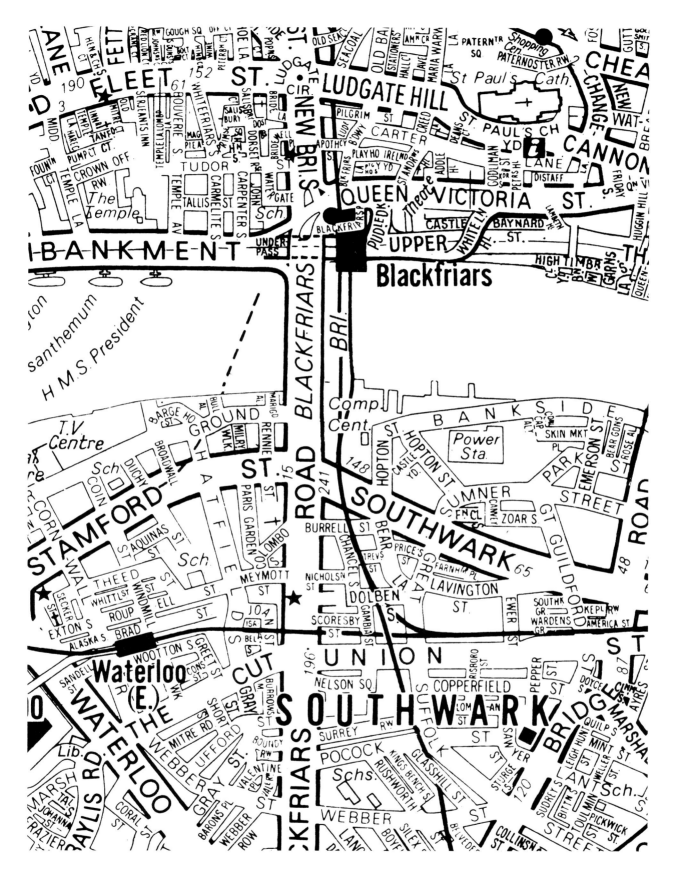

Reproduced by permission of Geographers' A-Z Map Co Ltd.

St. George's Fields

Glance from John Rocque's map of this section of London to the modern map and the change is clear: the fields of 250 years ago have been covered by roads and houses. Rocque carefully shows the trees and orchards; today this part of South London is dominated by its traffic routes.

St. George's Fields were named after the church of St. George the Martyr which dated back to the twelfth century and stood on the east side of Borough High Street just off the top right-hand corner of this map. The fields themselves were designated common land, meaning that at the time of Rocque's survey, Londoners enjoyed both grazing rights and the right to take firewood. However in 1768, reflecting the agricultural trend in favour of private property and against 'commons', these rights were extinguished.

The spaciousness of this area had ensured that over the centuries they had hosted a variety of activities, their wet and swampy nature delaying the onset of development. Soldiers had been trained here, the Lord Mayor of London met the returning Charles II and held a banquet in 1660, and six years later during the Great Fire, refugees from the City pitched their tents in the fields. St. George's Fields were also a well-known rallying point for tradesmen wishing to air grievances, many a petition of the seventeenth and eighteenth century having been first drawn up here.

Twelve years after the publication of Rocque's map, the new King's Bench prison was built in the north-east corner (2/9). One of the first inmates was the novelist Tobias Smollett who served three months in 1759 for libel, taking the opportunity to finish his novel *Sir Launcelot Greaves*. The politician John Wilkes was there between 1768 and 1770 for libel and obscenity, although he did not find his incarceration particularly irksome, making full use of the prison's shops and tennis courts and also being allowed visits from his numerous girlfriends. Wilkes' imprisonment was a political move by the government of the day, aimed at removing him from public life, but Wilkes simply addressed the crowds outside in St. George's Fields through his cell windows. On one occasion in May 1768 the watching soldiers panicked and fired on the bystanders, killing six people, an incident always referred to as 'the St. George's Fields Massacre'.

Burnt down in the Gordon riots of 1780 the King's Bench was rebuilt, and its succession of celebrities continued with the admission of Daniel Mendoza, a famous boxer who had fallen on hard times and proved unable to meet his debts, and after the Napoleonic wars it was the turn of the engineer Marc Isambard Brunel and his wife. Brunel was bailed out by means of a government grant of £5,000 largely obtained through the good offices of the Duke of Wellington. Marc's son Isambard Kingdom Brunel was one of the foremost Victorian engineers. The prison was finally demolished in the 1870s.

Rocque also shows Horsemonger Lane (2/9) where another gaol was to be constructed. Public executions took place on the roof of the building, as was memorably described by Charles Dickens in November 1849:

When the day dawned, thieves, low prostitutes, ruffians and vagabonds of every kind, flocked on to the ground, with every variety of offensive and foul behaviour. Fightings, faintings, whistlings, imitations of Punch, brutal jokes, tumultuous demonstrations of indecent delight when swooning women were dragged out of the crowd by the police with their dresses disordered, gave a new zest to the general entertainment. When the sun rose brightly – as it did – it gilded thousands upon thousands of upturned faces, so inexpressibly odious in their brutal mirth or callousness, that a man had cause to feel ashamed of the shape he wore, and to shrink from himself, as fashioned in the image of the devil.

Such a scene was no doubt commonplace at all the public executions which were held in Rocque's day.

St. George's Fields were also the scene for another notorious eighteenth-century protest, the Gordon Riots of 1780. The English Protestant Association had been formed in order to campaign against a bill going through Parliament which removed some of the political disabilities then placed on Catholics. On 2nd June the young Scottish peer Lord George Gordon rallied 60,000 of his supporters here near the Dog and Duck (4/2) before crossing Westminster Bridge to lobby MPs. A few days later the cry of 'No Popery!' turned into one of 'No Property!' and many shops and houses were looted, a frenzied scene depicted by Dickens in his novel *Barnaby Rudge*. By one of those ironies of history, the spot at which Gordon addressed his fanatical Protestants is today occupied by the Roman Catholic St. George's Cathedral. Gordon himself died in Newgate prison.

Rocque's map shows a number of inns in this area, including the Artichoke (3/9), the White Hart (11/1), the Horse Shoe (1/9) and the infamous Dog and Duck (4/2). This last had acquired its name because of the sport of duckhunting practised in the nearby ponds, but it also put on concerts as well as being the haunt of thieves and highwaymen. The Dog and Duck was finally suppressed by the magistrates in 1799. It was replaced by the Bethlem or Bedlam mental asylum which moved here in 1815 from London Wall; this institution in turn moved away in 1926 and the site now houses the Imperial War Museum. The gardens around it – the only remnants of St. George's Fields – were named by the newspaper proprietor Viscount Rothermere in honour of his mother.

The only other reminder of the fields is in the names of St. George's Circus, a busy roundabout today, and of St. George's Road which was Rocque's Lambeth Road (4/3). In 1771 an obelisk was place at the centre of the circus, with the results hinted at by Dickens in one of his *Christmas Stories:*

Those that are acquainted with London are aware of a locality on the Surrey side of the river Thames, called the Obelisk, or, more generally, the Obstacle.

By the beginning of the nineteenth century St. George's Fields had been almost completely built over, as a poem of 1813 lamented:

> Saint George's Fields are fields no more,
> The trowel supersedes the plough;
> Huge inundated swamps of yore
> Are changed to civic villas now.

The impetus behind the startling transformation of this part of South London came from the opening of the Westminster, Blackfriars and finally Waterloo Bridges.

Rocque's Newington Butts (7/7) is still that today, although the northern section is known as Newington Causeway: the name 'Newington' suggests that it had once been a New Town in the forest. Both roads followed the route of the old Roman road of Stane Street which led from London to Sussex. The triangular patch in the middle of the road marks our Elephant and Castle. There had once been a smithy here before it was taken over in 1760 by a coaching inn called the Elephant and Castle. From here the traveller took the Road to Camberwell (7/8), our Walworth Road, or the road to Clapham (11/6) which today is Kennington Park Road. Kennington Lane (10/4) is the same and one can just make out the interrupted Kennington Road on the western side. The openness of this district led several companies to erect almshouses in the vicinity, and Rocque puts in those of the Drapers (1/9) and the Fishmongers (6/7).

55

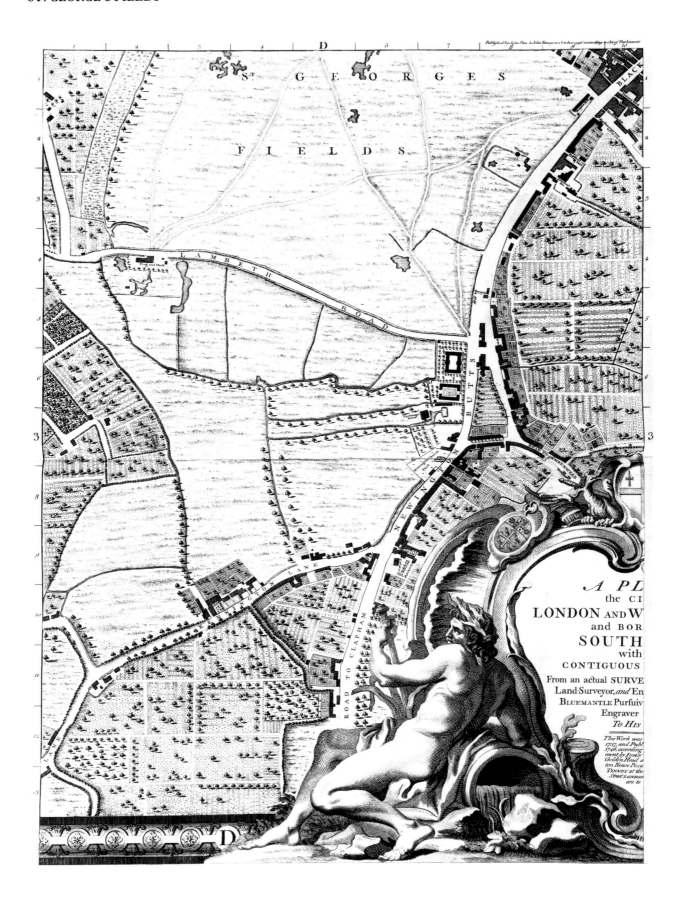

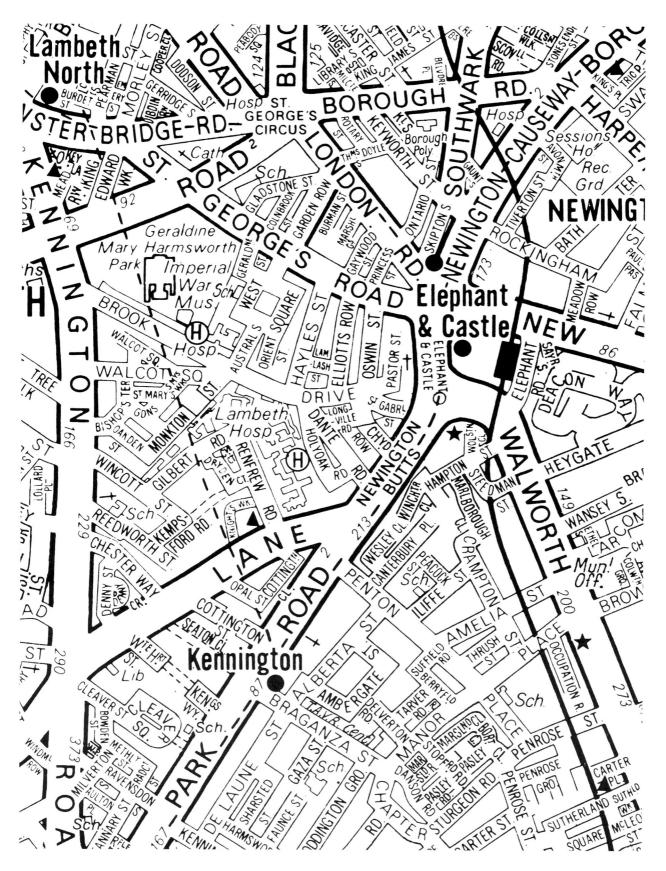

Reproduced by permission of Geographers' A-Z Map Co Ltd.

Moorgate and Shoreditch

Lying within and just outside the City, this area was already well developed by the early eighteenth century. Three gates are shown – Cripplegate, Moorgate and Bishopsgate – as well as the fields which stretch north out of the map and the crowded alleys and rookeries elsewhere, a testament to the detail of Rocque's surveying.

In the centre are the 'Moor Fields' (9/5), a last reminder of the medieval spaciousness which once marked this district. The chronicler Fitzstephen recorded how Londoners in the twelfth century used to walk out here from the City and skate on the frozen ice, play football and practise their archery. For centuries the marshy nature of these fields had inhibited building, but in the Georgian period the inexorable pace of expansion meant that soon after Rocque's map they were filled in and then built over. Remnants survive in the greenery of our Finsbury Square and Finsbury Circus.

By way of contrast the Artillery Ground (7/4) of the Honourable Artillery Company has survived intact. Beginning as the medieval Citizen Archers, they were later granted by Henry VIII a charter in 1537 as 'The Fraternity or Guild of Longbows, Crossbows and Handguns'. At first they trained at Artillery Lane in Spitalfields (10/10) but on falling out with the officers responsible for guarding the Tower of London they moved to this site. Their Artillery Ground also hosted some of the first cricket matches held in the eighteenth century, and it was from here that Lunardi made the first balloon ascent carried out in this country in September 1784. Huge crowds saw him off – but few witnessed him land forty miles away in Ware, Hertfordshire.

Tindal's Burying Ground (5/4) to the north of the Artillery Ground is now the nonconformist Bunhill Fields, the name coming from 'bones hill' – it had been intended as a plague pit in 1665. Several well-known people lie here, amongst them John Bunyan, William Blake and Daniel Defoe: the last had been buried in 1731 under the wrong name of 'Dubow'. Although it has been a public garden since 1869 the spiked gate to deter body-snatchers can still be seen. Rocque also shows a Quaker burial ground (5/3); George Fox, the founder of the Society of Friends, was buried here in 1690.

Another person who had been interred at Tindal's – in fact in 1742 at the time when Rocque was engaged on his survey – was Mrs. Susannah Wesley, mother of John, Charles and 17 other children. The reason for this is that on the other side of Royal Row, now City Road, can be seen the Methodist Meeting Hall (4/6) which was John Wesley's first headquarters. Ironically enough the building which he bought in 1739 for £115 and then converted had been a gun foundry. Wesley lived here with his mother until her death. By 1777 the old meeting place had proved too small and another chapel together with other buildings were erected a hundred yards to the west.

In the top right-hand corner of Rocque's map, the frequency of the name Holywell is explained by the existence of the priory of that name which was situated here until the Reformation. After its dissolution the neighbourhood housed an actors' colony. London's first two theatres had been built close by, the Theatre in Curtain Road (6/9) and the Curtain. In 1598 the Earl of Leicester's Men who occupied the Theatre fell out with the ground landlord and thereupon moved the whole enterprise down Bishopsgate, over London bridge and into Southwark where it formed the nucleus for the Globe – with consequences which can be seen in Rocque's map of Bankside.

Hoxton boasted two fine squares in the middle of the eighteenth century, Charles Square (2/6) and Hoxton Square (2/8). Born in the latter in 1755 was the future Dr. James Parkinson, the discoverer of the illness which bears his name. North of Hoxton, London petered out into fields and countryside, offering only a bowling green (1/7) and hence our Bowling Green Walk.

Over to the west beside Old Street is the church of St. Luke's (4/1), another product of the 50 New Churches Act and completed in 1733. The identity of the architect is still uncertain, but one of the major problems which he faced was the marshy site chosen for the church: in 1959 the elements finally won out and a portion of St. Luke's subsided. The church today is an empty shell.

On the other side of the road Rocque shows the overcrowded streets and alleys around Whitecross Street, noted for its market. Down the bottom is St. Giles, Cripplegate (10/1) and to its east the gate itself. The church in which Oliver Cromwell was married and John Milton buried, St. Giles was badly bombed during the 2nd World War but rebuilt it stands rather forlornly in the middle of the Barbican complex. The name Barbican comes from the barbican or Roman watch tower which stood here. In Rocque's day London Wall (11/3) would still have exhibited large sections of the original Roman wall built in the third century A.D. to protect the city. Nearby is Grub Street (9/3), home of Georgian London's 'hack writers': Pope lashed them in his *Dunciad*, Fielding wrote a play called *The Grub Street Opera*, and Oliver Goldsmith in *The Vicar of Wakefield* referred to it sarcastically as being 'the parent of excellence'.

The bottom lefthand corner emphasises yet again the number of churches in the City, amongst them being St. Alban's (12/1) and St. Michael's (12/2). St. Mary Aldermanbury (12/2) was transplanted to the United States after the 2nd World War, whilst St. Lawrence Jewry (13/2) has particular links with the City and derives its name from the Jewish community based here in the Middle Ages. Above it is Guildhall (12/2), for centuries the seat of the City's government.

On the north side of London Wall lies the Bethlem Hospital (11/5), better known as Bedlam and the place where for payment of a 2d entrance fee visitors could stare at the mentally disturbed inmates. Tom Rakewell finishes up here in the last plate of Hogarth's *The Rake's Progress*. In the early nineteenth century the Hospital moved away to St. George's Fields in South London. Another place of incarceration can be seen off Bishopsgate, the London Workhouse (11/8) built in 1698. Roy Porter gives the horrifying statistic, that of 2,339 children received into care here in the five years after 1750, only 168 were still alive in 1755[8].

At the junction of Bishopsgate with Wormwood and Camomile Streets is the gate (12/8), so named because it marked the route into the City used by the Bishops of London when journeying to and from their country residence in the little village of Bethnal Green. Leading off Bishopsgate is Houndsditch (13/10), the place where dogs were thrown during times of plague and when they were banned from the City. Two of the open spaces shown by Rocque in the bottom part of his survey remain with us today, although Devonshire Square (12/9) is smaller than it was 250 years ago. The other, Drapers' Gardens (13/5), marked the point at which the Great Fire stopped, halted by this natural fire-break. It is now a private garden attached to the Drapers' Hall. The church beside the Bishops' Gate is not surprisingly dedicated to St. Botolph (12/8), the patron saint of travellers.

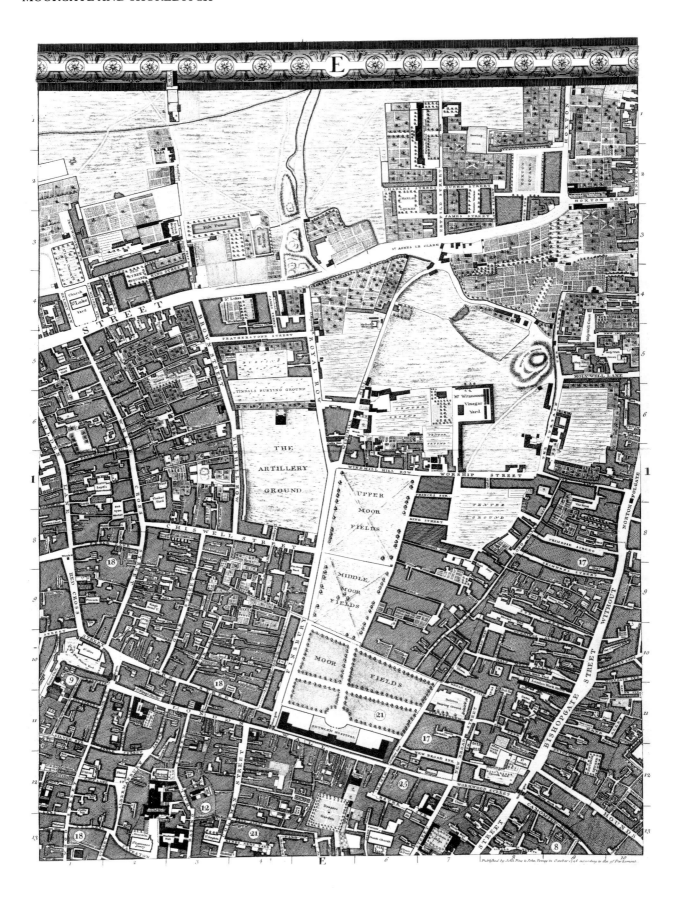

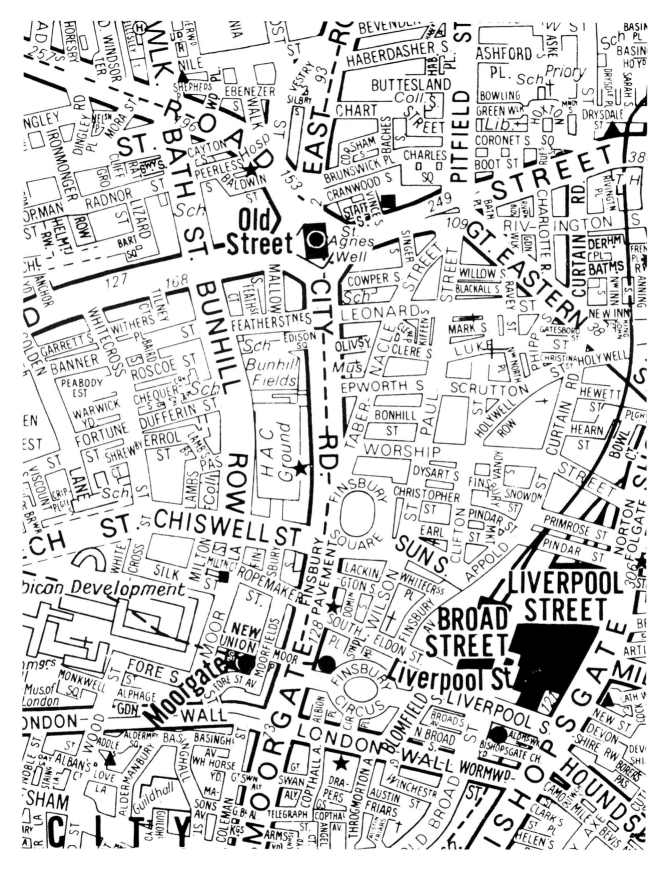

Reproduced by permission of Geographers' A-Z Map Co Ltd.

The City and Southwark

After the Great Fire of 1666 Christopher Wren prepared an overall plan for the rebuilding of the City of London, a set of proposals which if accepted would have resulted in a more formal London and dispensed with the less significant alleys and streets. As Rocque's map clearly shows, Wren's idea was turned down, leaving the City to grow up once more in a higgledy piggledy fashion – a large part of its charm which has even withstood the massive redevelopment since the 1960s.

One testimonial to the Fire does however remain securely with us: the Monument itself (5/6). Designed by Wren and put up between 1671 and 1677, in Rocque's day it still carried the inscription which blamed 'Popish frenzy, which wrought such horrors' for the outbreak of the fire. Not until 1830 was this offensive and quite untrue passage removed. Just to the east of the Monument is the infamous Pudding Lane, site of the small baker's shop in which a blaze on the night of 1st September 1666 eventually led to the destruction of four-fifths of the City of London.

Much of eighteenth-century life was conducted out in the open streets. Few shops existed and most people were dependent upon local markets for the purchase of their provisions – without fridges or freezers nothing could be stored for very long. Cheapside (1/1) was the venue of one of the most important of these markets, and the names of the streets leading off it even today indicate the kind of goods on offer: Wood Street, Honey Lane, Bread Street and Milk Street. Further along was Poultry (2/3) and then Leadenhall Market (2/7). As famous as any was the Billingsgate Fish Market (6/7) down by the Thames. Renowned for its bad language almost as much as for its fish, the market moved away to the Isle of Dogs in 1981. Fishmongers Hall (6/5) was and still is on the other side of London Bridge. The existence of the Customs House (7/9) underlines London's role as a port.

Rocque also shows in his survey the number and prominence of the City churches with virtually one on every street-corner. Perhaps the most famous was St. Mary-le-Bow on Cheapside (2/2) whose 'Bow Bells' used to ring out the curfew in the Middle Ages. Its name originated in the Norman 'bow' arches which can still be seen in the crypt, despite extensive damage to the church in 1666 and again in 1941. One church in this section which did survive the Great Fire was Great St. Helen's beside Bishopsgate (1/8), whilst another was St. Olave's, Hart Street (4/9): the latter was Samuel Pepys' 'regular' and he lies buried in the chancel with his wife Elizabeth. As the fire approached St. Olave's in 1666, Pepys himself ordered the wooden shacks and buildings which at that time clustered around every church to be pulled down, thus saving St. Olave's from joining the conflagration. Allhallows, Barking (6/10) was not so fortunate, but the tower from which Pepys watched the initial stages of the Great Fire remains, even though the church was again badly damaged during the Blitz. Of St. Dunstan's in the East (5/8) only the shell has survived.

Mention of 'the City' today rightly conjures up associations of finance and business, and Rocque's map shows both the Bank of England (2/4), founded in 1694, and the Royal Exchange (2/5) which had developed as a place where merchants could meet in order to discuss trade. In the eighteenth century the Bank of England suffered from periodic crises of confidence: on 'Black Friday', 1746, it nearly went bust itself. The Lord Mayor's Mansion House (2/4) is also on the same site today as it was 250 years ago. Much eighteenth-century wheeling and dealing was carried on at the numerous coffee houses in the vicinity, for example in what Rocque calls 'Exchange Alley' between Cornhill and Lombard Street (2/5).

Comparing the two maps of the City it is notable that there have been few major road improvements in the City since the 1740s – unlike most other areas surveyed by Rocque – simply because any development was fraught with costly complications. Cannon Street, Lombard Street and Upper and Lower Thames Street

have all been widened, but only King William Street is completely new, built in the 1830s as the approach road to the new London Bridge.

In Rocque's map it is Fish Street Hill by the Monument which leads to the bridge. This, 'old' London Bridge, dated back to the twelfth century. When it was first built, the stone bridge was regarded as one of the wonders of Europe, but as London had grown so had this bridge proved increasingly inadequate to cope with the increasing volume of traffic. In the 1830s John Rennie finally constructed a new London Bridge, slightly to the west of the old. Rennie's bridge is now in the United States, replaced by the present bridge put up in the 1960s.

The south bank of the Thames was here relatively developed by the middle of the eighteenth century, mainly because it catered for the travellers passing into and out of the City who had to use the Borough. Lining this street on the east side had been taverns and inns, including the Tabard from which Chaucer's pilgrims had set off. Unfortunately Southwark had its own Great Fire in 1676 and only the galleried The George (10/3) now suggests their former character. Unable to compete with the coming of the railway – London Bridge station, the capital's first, was opened only a hundred yards away in 1836 – many of the inns shut down and only the names of several alleys such as King's Head Yard and White Hart Yard provide a reminder of their past existence.

Like the City on the other side of the river, Borough High Street was in Rocque's time a ceaseless hive of activity. There was the annual Southwark Fair held near St. Margaret's Hill (10/3) and also the daily Borough market, both severely disrupting the traffic. The market was moved off the road in 1756 and has survived to this day as dealing in wholesale fruit and vegetables; Southwark Fair was stopped completely in 1762.

Old London Bridge with the shops and houses still in place; this view is looking west and therefore St. Magnus the Martyr and the Monument are just visible on the right.

Of Southwark's churches Rocque shows St. Saviour's (9/4) which is now Southwark Cathedral. Although always on this site, this is its third name, having been founded in 1106 as St. Mary Overie (or 'Over the Water'). There is another St. Olave's (8/6) too: the reason for the frequency of the name 'Olaf' in this neighbourhood is that King Olaf had helped the English to defeat the Danes here at the Battle of London Bridge in 1014. This church was pulled down in 1928; St. George's (13/2) has survived but not St. John's (12/10).

Southwark's other claims to notoriety centred on its entertainment resorts, its hospitals and its prisons. Regarding the first, in the Middle Ages London's brothels or 'stews' were on this side of the river. The land was in fact owned by the Bishops of Winchester which was why the girls were known as 'Winchester geese'. Most of the Elizabethan playhouses were also near: by straining one's eyes one can just see Globe Alley (8/2) where the Globe was situated between 1599 and 1644. By Rocque's day, however, both brothels and theatres had moved elsewhere. As for the hospitals, St. Thomas's (9/4) had been originally attached to St. Mary Overie; it moved to Lambeth when London Bridge station was extended in 1856. Guy's (10/4), founded in 1721 by the bookseller Thomas Guy, is still there.

Southwark's prisons also clustered around the Borough. One was the privately run gaol in Clink Street (8/3) for the use of the Bishops of Winchester, and there were also the King's Bench (13/3) and the Marshalsea (12/3). When John Wesley visited the latter in 1753 he described it in his *Journal* as 'a nursery of all manner of wickedness. Oh shame to man that there should be such a place, such a picture of hell upon earth!'

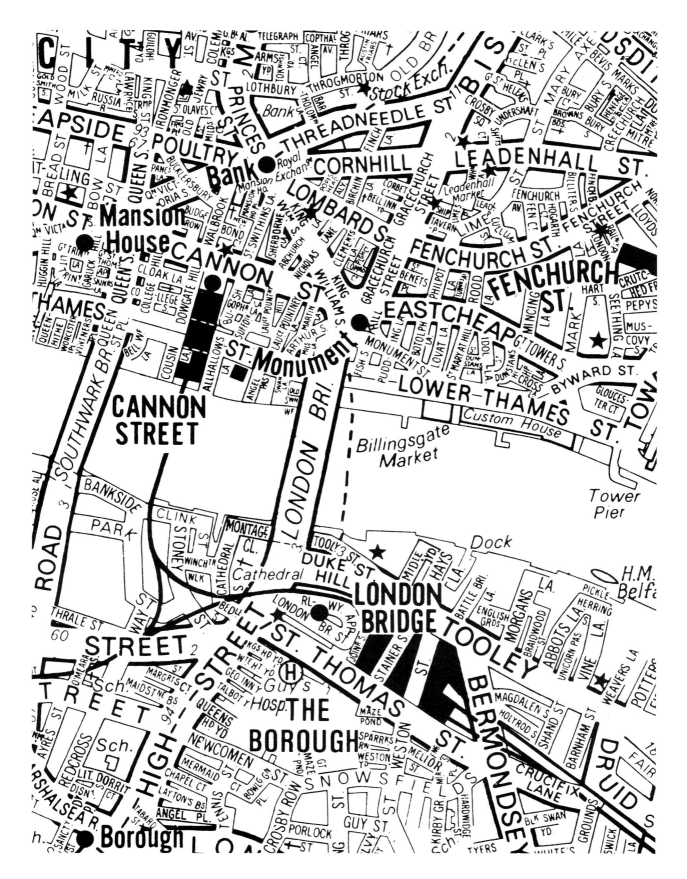

Reproduced by permission of Geographers' A-Z Map Co Ltd.

Bermondsey and the Old Kent Road

As is the case with all of South London in the 1740s other than the built-up section around Southwark, Rocque's map emphasises the rural character of this area. The only parts that can be called residential were in the top left-hand corner just off Borough High Street, the densely populated strips along the northern end of Kent Street, and the village in the other corner centred on the neighbourhood where Bermondsey Abbey had once stood.

The abbey's origins dated back to 1082 when it was founded as a monastery by some Cluniac monks before moving up the religious hierarchy and becoming a priory and finally, in 1399, an abbey. In terms both of its size and its landholdings, Bermondsey Abbey was a wealthy establishment. Its western tip had started at King John's Court (2/9), stretching eastwards between Long Walk and Grange Walk into the next section. Like London's other abbeys, priories and monasteries it was dissolved during the Reformation of the 1530s and 1540s, the buildings being largely pulled down before the remnants were finally converted into Bermondsey House by Sir Thomas Pope in 1541, a mansion with a 20-acre garden. This in turn was eventually demolished: nothing remains of either house or abbey except that the latter's outline can still be traced – Bermondsey Square for instance marks the inner courtyard of the abbey – and the hinges of one of its gates are visible today in Grange Walk.

Like all medieval religious houses Bermondsey Abbey was the focus of its neighbouring community, providing jobs for the villagers as well as keeping an eye on its spiritual well-being. Close to the abbey was a chapel first referred to in a document of 1296: 'Mary Magdalen chapel is in the hands of the Prior and Convent of Bermondsey'. It would have been used by the laymen working for the monks. The chapel escaped the ravages of the Reformation but had become so rundown by 1680 that it had to be rebuilt – it is this church (2/9) which is shown by Rocque and is today the parish church of St. Mary Magdalen. Parts of the tower are medieval.

Inside the church the churchwardens' pew can still be seen, equipped with a curtain so that the wardens could transact parish business away from the public gaze. The walls are lined with hatchments which were the paintings placed over the door of the deceased, brought to the church for the funeral and then left there. Only the wealthy could afford such an outlay, and the number of hatchments in St. Mary Magdalen underlines the fact that until the Victorian period Bermondsey was rather a fashionable part of London, being almost a garden suburb after the Great Fire – an impression confirmed by the old houses in Bermondsey Street (2/9) which have survived up to the present. Rocque also shows a school in the King's Road (3/9), now Grange Road. Founded by Josiah Bacon in 1703 for sixty boys, the site now houses an Institute of Adult Education.

Apart from the market gardens once tended by the monks and still in the mid-eighteenth century prominent in Bermondsey, the main source of employment was provided by the tanning industry, the yards of which are represented lining the northern side of Long Lane (2/7). Granted a royal charter in 1703, tanning had established itself here because the area was close to the river Thames and thus the plentiful supplies of water always needed for that occupation. Long Lane was so called because in medieval times it had indeed been the long lane leading from London Bridge to Bermondsey Abbey.

Otherwise the main feature of Rocque's map is the highway of Kent Street running diagonally down towards the south. Continuing out of this map it became the Old Kent Road. This was the only thoroughfare between London and Europe, which meant that many famous incidents and processions had taken place along its route: the victorious Henry V marched up here after the Battle of Agincourt; Jack Cade and his 40,000 Kentish rebels made their way along it in July 1450 to capture London – later a piece of Cade's corpse came back down this way for exhibition at Blackheath; and Charles II and his followers proceeded up Kent Street in 1660 en route to reclaim the throne. Such a volume of traffic explains the number of inns dotting the way, such as the Harp (4/5), the Bull (5/5), the White Horse (6/8) and the Castle (7/9).

The already narrow Kent Street (3/4) was fringed on both sides by tightly packed and squalid dwellings – hence Rocque's thick black lines – which were distinguished by the number of thieves and robbers who resided there, as well as by the pigs and donkeys kept inside most of the houses themselves. The eighteenth-century novelist Tobias Smollett called Kent Street 'a most disgraceful entrance to such an opulent city. A foreigner, in passing this beggarly and ruinous suburb, conceives such an idea of misery and meanness, as all the wealth and magnificence of London and Westminster are afterwards unable to destroy. A friend of mine who brought a Parisian from Dover in his own post-chaise, contrived to enter Southwark when it was dark, that his friend might not perceive the nakedness of this quarter.' Even in the middle of the Victorian era Dickens was still able to call Kent Street 'the worst kept part of London – in a police sense, of course – excepting the Haymarket'. In *David Copperfield* David leaves London by foot down this road on his way to his aunt Betsey Trotwood in Dover.

In fact the road referred to by Dickens was no longer the only thoroughfare from Kent. In 1814 Kent Street had been bypassed by the new Great Dover Street, and Kent Street was eventually renamed Tabard Street. The 'One Mile Stone' (5/6) shown by Rocque – one mile to London Bridge – is now the spot at which our New Kent Road meets Great Dover Street and Tower Bridge Road: in the 1740s New Kent Road was not even a path.

Lock Fields derived its name from the ancient 'Loke' hospital (4/5) founded in the fourteenth century for the care of lepers – the word 'loke' is thought to have come from the Saxon log or loc meaning 'shut' or 'closed'. In Henry VIII's reign several other 'Lock' or leper hospitals were also set up on the outskirts of the City. This Lock hospital was closed down in 1760. Of Lock Fields themselves barely a blade of grass still remains, the nineteenth-century march of London pushing on and through them down towards the south. A glance at the modern map shows the maze of roads and streets which now cover Rocque's fields and gardens. Mr. Wemmick in Dickens' *Great Expectations* lived with his father, the 'aged parent', in Walworth in 'a little wooden cottage in the midst of plots of garden' – but not for much longer.

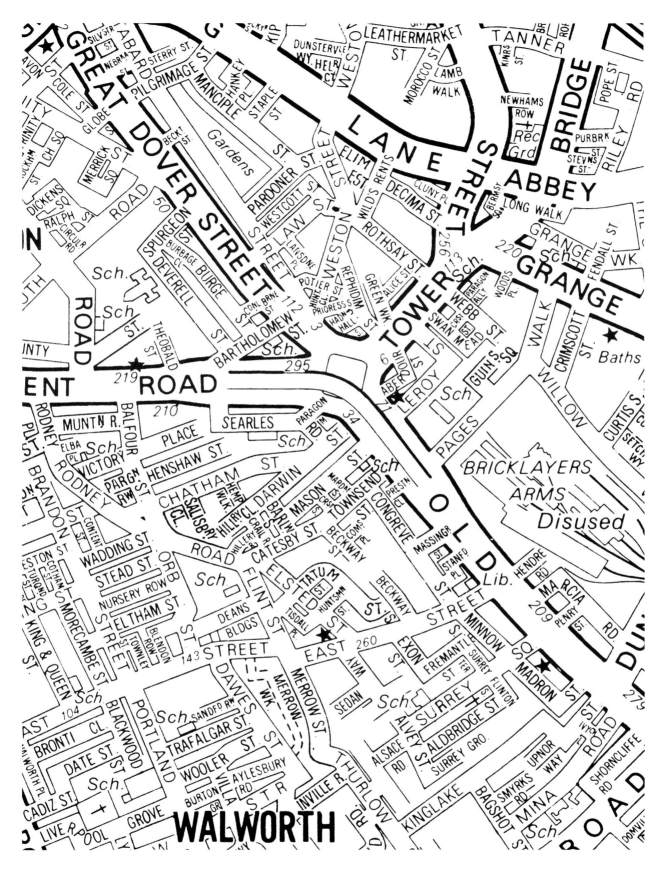

Reproduced by permission of Geographers' A-Z Map Co Ltd.

Spitalfields and Whitechapel

In the Middle Ages Spitalfields was made up of farmland and fields, a favourite spot in which residents of the crowded City could stroll and take the country air. By Rocque's day, however, it was beginning to be built on and over. And yet, unlike the western parts of London, it was not the wealthy and powerful who were moving into this area. One major reason behind this was that the system of land tenure differed as between the ends of London: in the west long leases were obtainable, thus encouraging the fashionable to build splendid mansions, but in East London leases were normally granted on a 21-year term which was too short for the erection of buildings intended for future generations. As a result this district catered for the less affluent, often attracted here anyway by the fact that it lay outside the jurisdiction of the City guilds, a magnet in particular for foreigners.

The first influx had come in the years after 1685 when Louis XIV revoked the Edict of Nantes, forcing thousands of Huguenots to flee the country, John Rocque's parents amongst them. Those that came to London settled mainly in Soho and Spitalfields with smaller communities in Wandsworth and Marylebone. The Huguenots in Spitalfields were predominantly silkweavers and several of their houses in Church, now Fournier, Street (10/3) with the long attic windows are today being renovated. Spittle Square (8/1), now unrecognisable from Rocque's day, was also inhabited by the more prosperous Huguenot weavers. They had their own place of worship too, a chapel built in 1743 on the corner of Church Street and Brick Lane (9/4). Now a mosque, it has also served as a Methodist chapel and synagogue. The weavers liked to have caged birds near them as they worked, their songs breaking up the monotonous hum of the looms: thus Club Row (5/3) specialised in the sale of such creatures.

The two sure indications of a growing community are amply borne out in Rocque's map: markets and churches. Regarding the first, Charles II granted a charter for Spitalfields market in 1682 (9/2). Rebuilt in

the 1920s it is still on the same site handling fruit and vegetables. Also in the bottom left-hand corner is Petticoat Lane (12/1). Once called Hog Lane because of the pigs quartered in the adjacent fields, its official name today is Middlesex Street. The business of selling and dealing in second-hand clothes seems to have grown up over the centuries but really took off in the Victorian period with the arrival of thousands of Jewish people.

Of the district's churches, the largest is undoubtedly Christ Church (10/3) whose spire still dominates the horizon. Built here under the 50 New Churches Act because the authorities were disturbed by what they saw as the spread of immorality and atheism in the vicinity, Hawksmoor's church was finished in 1729. To the north is St. Matthew's, Bethnal Green (4/7), completed in 1745 just before the publication of Rocque's map. As with Christ Church, there were social and political reasons explaining its construction: the Act of Parliament passed to 'compleat the Church at Bethnal Green and pay debts already contracted' had begun:

> Whereas the want of a place for public worship of Almighty God hath been a great cause of increase of dissoluteness of morals and a disregard for religion, too apparent in the younger and poorer sort . . .

Despite the completion of St. Matthew's, the churchyard in the eighteenth century was a famed venue for bull-running sessions. Although the church's interior was destroyed in 1940, St. Matthew's was carefully restored.

The architect of St. Matthew's, George Dance, responsible for the Mansion House in the City, had just rebuilt another church in this area, St. Leonard's Shoreditch (3/1). There had been a church on this site for hundreds of years, but the building of the early eighteenth century had suddenly disintegrated during a service in December 1716:

70

the walls of the old church rent asunder, with a frightful sound; and a considerable amount of mortar falling, the congregation fled on all sides to the doors, where they severely injured each other by their efforts to escape.

Work started on the new St. Leonard's in 1736 but had to be halted that summer because of anti-Irish riots, local people being incensed that their jobs had been taken by cheaper labour from Ireland. The militia from the Tower of London finally put down the disturbances and the church was finished in 1740.

The other church shown by Rocque, St. Mary's in Whitechapel (12/6), also had a long history. Founded in the thirteenth century the chapel had been conspicuous for its whitewash covering – and thus the name 'Whitechapel'. In the seventeenth century a certain Richard Brandon, hangman, was buried in the churchyard: Brandon it was who had cut off the head of Charles I in 1649. In 1710 a celebrated controversy spilled over into the church when the vicar took the opportunity of a new altar-piece being installed to portray one of his theological enemies as Judas Iscariot. Crowds flocked to St. Mary's before the Bishop of London ordered the painting to be removed. Badly damaged by German bombs St. Mary's was pulled down after the 2nd World War and its site is now a public garden.

Apart from its weavers and market traders, Spitalfields' other main occupation centred on the brewing firm Truman's which was based at the Black Eagle Brewery in Brick Lane (8/3). Still there today, several of the buildings which are visible from the street date back to Rocque's time. Originally the smells emanating from the brewery would have floated off into the fields, but by the 1740s the increasingly residential neighbourhood had to put up with the pungent odours – another reason why the fashionable

migrated westwards rather than to the east where so many of London's more noxious industries were located.

As early as the eighteenth century parts of East London had turned into rookeries and slums, often used as hideaways by thieves and highwaymen. The notorious criminal Jack Sheppard had been born in White Row (10/2) in 1702. Part of the problem was that work in the weaving trade was seasonal, and a spell of mourning at court could lead to a sharp decline in orders and therefore destitution. Mulberry trees had failed to root in Spitalfields, which meant that the weavers were dependent on foreign supplies. In the nineteenth century French competition virtually wiped out the native silkweaving business. The Victorians built roads through some of the worst sections, as was the case with Commercial Street in 1848. Even then the arrival of Jewish refugees in the late nineteenth century was still to happen.

But in Rocque's time this area still retained many reminders of its recent rural past. Both Bethnal Green and Hackney were no more than hamlets some distance from London: the Road to Hackney (2/2) is now Hackney Road and Cock Lane (5/3), which Rocque shows petering out into little more than a farm track, is Bethnal Green Road. These fields were much used by highwaymen. Whitechapel Street down at the bottom is more comparable with today's route, its width explained by its use as a route for drovers herding in their animals from East Anglia. But even here the 'Field Gate' (11/8) is precisely what its name suggests. On the corner opposite was the Whitechapel Bell Foundry; founded in 1570 on the north side of the street it moved here in 1738 and survives to this day.

Of all the areas surveyed by John Rocque probably none have experienced quite so many far-reaching cultural transformations as this part of London.

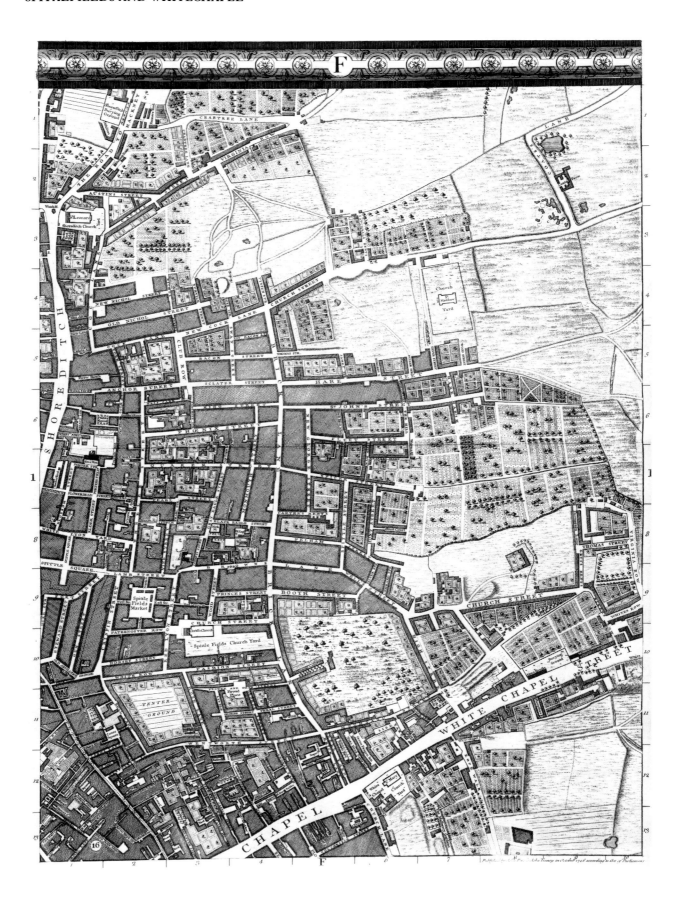

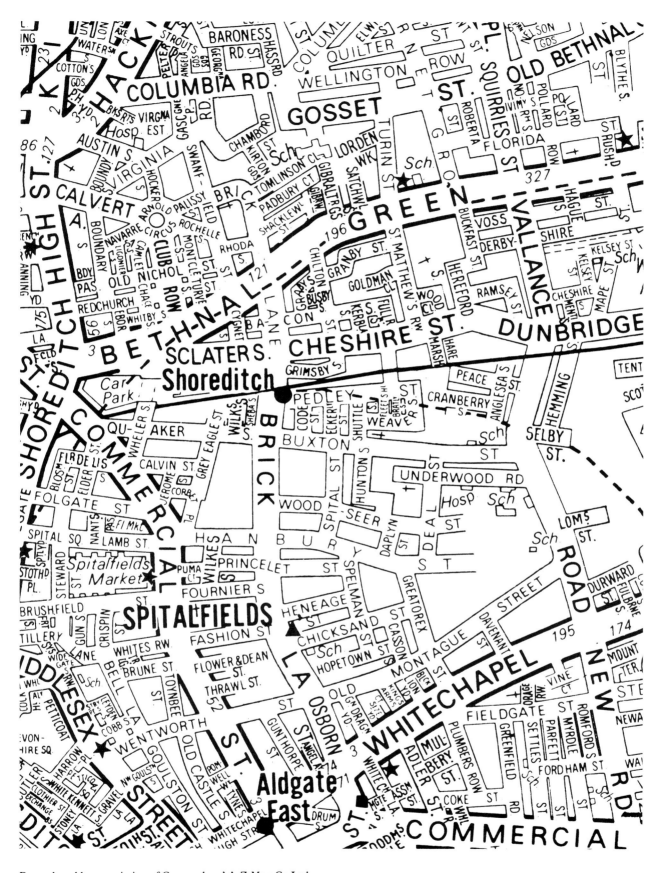

Reproduced by permission of Geographers' A-Z Map Co Ltd.

The Tower of London and Bermondsey

This central section of Rocque's map is dominated by the Tower of London (7/2). Built at the command of William the Conqueror, it had been used by the Normans as a means of intimidating the recalcitrant native Londoners. Over the centuries the Tower had fulfilled many other roles such as those of ammunition dump, repository of the Crown Jewels, prison and royal zoo. In 1666 the Great Fire nearly reached the White Tower which was then packed with gunpowder. The diarist John Evelyn estimated that if it had done so the explosion

would undoubtedly have not only beaten down and destroyed all the Bridge, but sunk and torn all the vessels in the river and rendered the demolition beyond all expression for several miles even about the country.

In fact the pulling down of the nearby houses halted the blaze although it did reach the moat of the Tower. As for the animals once kept here, in 1834 they were transferred away to form the basis of the Regent's Park Zoo.

On the north-west side of the Tower lies Tower Hill (6/1) where the influential and powerful were executed: Tyburn was reserved for 'the common people'. The scaffold stood here from the fourteenth century up to the middle of the eighteenth: the last execution took place the year after Rocque's map was published when Lord Lovat was beheaded in 1747 – at least Lovat had the satisfaction of seeing a stand containing 1,000 spectators collapse under their weight.

In the Middle Ages the fields around the Tower were scattered with religious houses which although dissolved during Henry VIII's reign had left behind their names: the Minories, for example, derives from the nuns called the 'Minoresses' or Little Sisters once based here and Crutched Friars (4/1) from the friars with crosses on their chests. One religious foundation which did survive was the Royal Foundation of St. Katharine, established by Queen Matilda in 1146. Being under the personal patronage of the Queen it

escaped the fate experienced by other priories and monasteries during the Reformation; Rocque clearly shows the church (8/4).

Because the medieval religious houses offered rights of sanctuary the neighbourhood around the Tower was something of a criminal ghetto, as is hinted at by the number of alleys apparent in the 1740s. Defoe's Moll Flanders was here briefly before being 'filled with horror at the place I was in'; she moved on elsewhere. The poverty of the area was exacerbated by the continuous arrival of immigrants who usually landed at Irongate Stairs (8/3): those who could afford to pushed on out of East London, leaving behind the residue who remained here because of the district's cheap food and accommodation; nor did the jurisdiction of the City guilds apply. The poorer Jewish people, often the Ashkenaze, lived in the aptly named Poor Jewry Lane (3/1) and the more wealthy Sephardi were based around Guildhall further west. Other migrants included the Irish who controlled the rag trade centred on Rosemary Lane (5/4), a street also specialising in the handling of stolen goods.

Pockets of countryside remain in this section, among them Goodman's Fields (3/4) with the Tenter Ground in the middle – hence today's Tenter Streets. At the time of Rocque's survey there was also a Goodman's Fields Theatre in Lemon or Leman Street (3/5). The young David Garrick first made his name here in October 1741 as Shakespeare's Richard III. So enormous was the acclaim for Garrick's performance that one observer commented that 'There are a dozen dukes of a night at Goodman's Fields sometimes.' Throughout the winter of 1741-42 Garrick's presence ensured that this little East London theatre was the most fashionable place in town, much to the annoyance of the proprietors of Drury Lane and Covent Garden theatre, who finally had their unlicensed rival closed down in May 1742. It was never to reopen but Garrick himself went on to find fame and considerable fortune, leaving an estate worth more than £100,000.

The area in the top left-hand corner of the map is Aldgate, named after the gate which still spanned the High Street (2/1). Close by was the church of St. Botolph, rebuilt during the years of Rocque's survey. Daniel Defoe had been married in the church that was pulled down; in his *Journal of the Plague Year*, Defoe graphically described the plague pits sited in Aldgate in 1665. To the south of Cable Street is Wellclose Square with the Danish church in the middle (5/7). Ned Ward described its congregation in scathing terms:

Their uncomb'd locks, tobacco breaths, and seafaring apparel, added such further fragrancy to the former (smell of pitch and tar) that no rats that had taken sanctuary in a Cheshire cheese could have smelt more frowzily.

Another group of Scandinavian immigrants, the Swedes, also had their own church (5/9).

The riverside swarmed with scores of alehouses, dancing rooms and brothels catering for the amusement of the offduty sailor, particularly around the notorious Wapping High Street (11/8). However, as Rocque also shows, there was the parish church of St. John (11/9) which was to be rebuilt in 1760 on the other side of the road. Bombed in the 2nd World War, only its shell now remains.

But if Rocque shows an East London which was already overcrowded and poverty-stricken in parts, the major transformation was still to come. By the early nineteenth century the expansion of Britain's overseas trade encouraged the dock companies to construct huge enclosed docks, sheltering behind high walls. One of the first was the London Docks, situated in what had once been fields and effectively isolating Wapping from the rest of London. Further upstream St. Katharine's Docks were built, an operation which in the 1820s required the clearance of over 11,000 people. If the docks did provide employment for some

of the thousands of families flooding into the East End it was a dependence that was certain to cause problems if the docks ever closed down – as of course they did in the late 1960s.

The number of stairs on both sides of the river underlines that in the 1740s it was quicker to cross the Thames by means of a waterman, even if his language was often vehemently abusive, than to try and use the congested London Bridge. Tower Bridge, the last of the bridges to be built over the Thames, was not completed until 1894.

The south side of the Thames shows Bermondsey, an area with many similarities to its counterpart Wapping. Both were often flooded at high tide and the streets facing the river were occupied by perhaps the poorest of all Londoners. In his *Oliver Twist* of 1838 Charles Dickens described riverside Bermondsey as

the filthiest, the strangest, the most extraordinary of the many localities that are hidden in London, wholly unknown, even by name, to the great mass of its inhabitants . . . in such a neighbourhood, beyond dockhead, in the Borough of Southwark, stands Jacob's Island.

In Rocque's map this stands at (13/5).

This district had not always been poor: the Order of St. John of Jerusalem had once owned land here, from which came St. John at Thames and then Shad Thames (11/3). Redriff (now Bermondsey) Wall was erected as a makeshift barrier in order to hold back the river. Otherwise this southern bank was crammed with wharves and warehouses which stored much of the foodstuffs brought to London, thus earning Bermondsey the nickname of 'London's larder'. As with East London it was the Victorian period which saw Bermondsey's fields and gardens covered with factories and cheap housing.

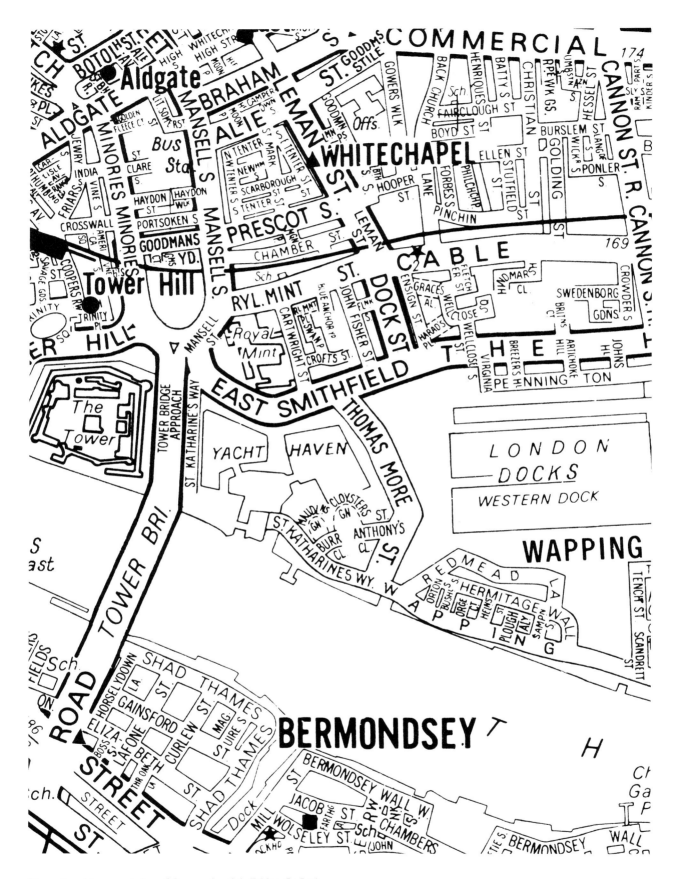

Reproduced by permission of Geographers' A-Z Map Co Ltd.

Bermondsey

Looking at John Rocque's map it is difficult to believe that this district is now an integral part of South London. Rocque shows trees, fields and market gardens; today's map is dominated by both major and minor roads. In the 1740s there was only a little development in the top left-hand corner based around Grange Walk (3/2) which had once marked the eastern boundary of Bermondsey Abbey. Three Tanner's Yards are shown, underlining the importance of tanning as Bermondsey's staple industry.

The rural character of eighteenth-century Bermondsey attracted Londoners wishing to stretch their legs in congenial surroundings as well as to visit the pleasure gardens and resorts dotted around the neighbourhood. The most famous was that near Cherry Garden (1/10), to which Samuel Pepys took his wife and maids in April 1667:

Over the water to the Jamaica house, where I never was before, and then the girls did run wagers on the bowling-green, and there with much pleasure spent but little, and so home.

Rocque's 'Rope Makers Walk' (4/5) was soon to be the site of Bermondsey Spa, opened in 1770. William Addison in his *English Spas*[9] noted that

The owner of the gardens when the spring was discovered in 1770 was Thomas Keyse, the artist, who made use of them for displaying his paintings, and exercised his talent to good effect in furnishing and decorating the music-room.

Quite apart from the orchestra and picture gallery Keyse once painted a large picture model of the Siege of Gibraltar in order to attract customers, an enormous undertaking in view of the fact that the model covered four acres. However after Keyse's death the popularity of Bermondsey Spa waned and it was closed down in 1804, leaving behind only its name in Spa Road.

At the bottom of Rocque's map is 'The Kent Road' (12/4), the main highway from London to Kent and then France. Chaucer's pilgrims would have come down this way to Canterbury, the traditional first stop being the well of St. Thomas à Watering, a spring dedicated to Becket which lay just off the bottom of this map. Perhaps by then the pilgrims had begun to recover from the effects of the hospitality which they had doubtless enjoyed in the inns on Borough High Street. As Chaucer's Miller puts it:

if the words get muddled in my tale
Just put it down to too much Southwark ale.

The Kent Road had seen many famous marches and processions over the centuries, but perhaps none more splendid than the return of Charles II in 1660, described by the diarist John Evelyn:

This day (May 29th) came in his Majestie Charles the 2nd to London after a sad, and long Exile, and Calamitous Suffering both of the King and Church: being 17 yeares: This was also his Birthday, and with a Triumph of above 20000 horse and foote, brandishing their swords and shouting with unexpressable joy: The wayes straw'd with flowers, the bells ringing, the streets hung with Tapissry, fountaines running with wine: The Mayor, Aldermen, all the Companies in their liver(ie)s, Chaines of Gold, banners; Lords and nobles, Cloth of Silver, gold and vellvet every body clad in, the windos and balconies all set with Ladys, Trumpets, Musick, and (myriads) of people flocking the streetes and was as far as Rochester, so as they were 7 hours in passing the Citty, even from 2 in the afternoone 'til nine at night: I stood in the strand, and beheld it, and blessed God: And all this without one drop of bloud, and by that very army, which rebell'd against him: but it was the Lords doing . . . for such a Restauration was never seene in the mention of any history, antient or modern, since the returne of the Babylonian Captivity, nor so joyfull a day, and so bright, ever seene in this nation: this hapning when to expect or effect it, was past all humane policy.

In Charles Dickens' *A Tale of Two Cities* there is a graphic description of the mail coach making its laborious way to Dover:

There was a steaming mist in all the hollows, and it had roamed in its forlornness up the hill, like an evil spirit, seeking rest and finding none. A clammy and intensely cold mist, it made its slow way through the air in ripples that visibly followed and overspread one another, as the waves on an unwholesome sea might do.

This helps to explain the number of strategically placed taverns noted by Rocque: the Greyhound (9/2), the Bull and Butcher (6/3) and the Blue Anchor (8/10) – thus our Blue Anchor Street. More gruesomely, because the Kent Road was used by so many travellers the authorities often displayed the remains of executed criminals beside the road as a reminder of the importance of good behaviour. In 1740 for instance, whilst Rocque was carrying out his survey, he might well have come across the quarters of a father and son both found guilty of murder.

Some of our modern roads can be seen on the old map. The unnamed passageway running parallel with the Kent Road to the north is Rolls Road, called after the Rolls family who held land here in the eighteenth century. The road outside the Greyhound is Dunton Road. Blue Anchor Road is now Southwark Park Road – the park itself is in the adjoining section. Neckinger Road (2/4) is our Abbey Street. The name 'Neckinger' is a corruption of the words 'Devil's neckerchief', a reference to the pirates hanged near here, and was originally called after the river flowing through the district, a supply of water vital both to Bermondsey Abbey and as the basis of the area's industry, as Edward Walford explained: 'The Neckinger was formerly navigable, for small craft, from the Thames to the abbey precincts, and gives name to the Neckinger

Road. When the abbey was destroyed, and the ground passed into the possession of others, the houses which were built on the site still received a supply of water from this water-course. In process of time tanneries were established on the spot, most probably on account of the valuable supply of fresh water obtaining every twelve hours from the river.'

As with the rest of London it was the Victorian period which transformed this section, causing an enormous growth in population. It was a growth fuelled by the railways whose lines ploughed through the fields and gardens depicted by Rocque. The Bricklayers' Arms station for instance was opened in 1844 at the back of where the Greyhound (9/2) had once stood. Dickens in *Our Mutual Friend* wrote of

that district of the flat country tending to the Thames, where Kent and Surrey meet, and where the railways still bestride the market-gardens that will soon die under them.

The station was later used for the conveyance of sheep and cattle but is now disused.

Apart from the leather industry, this part of Bermondsey was very dependent economically on the local factory of Peek Freans, the biscuit manufacturers, which began in Drummond Road in 1857 and which is still there today. Churches too were needed: hence St. James's just by Old Jamaica Road, built in 1829, which can hold nearly 2,000 people and was a 'Waterloo' church, and St. Anne's Thorburn Square of 1869.

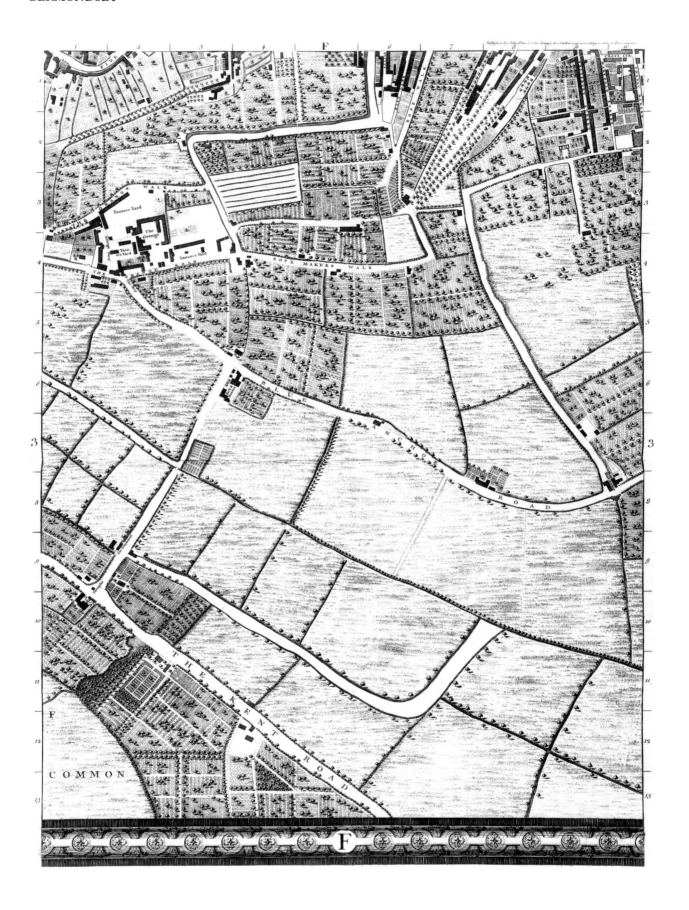

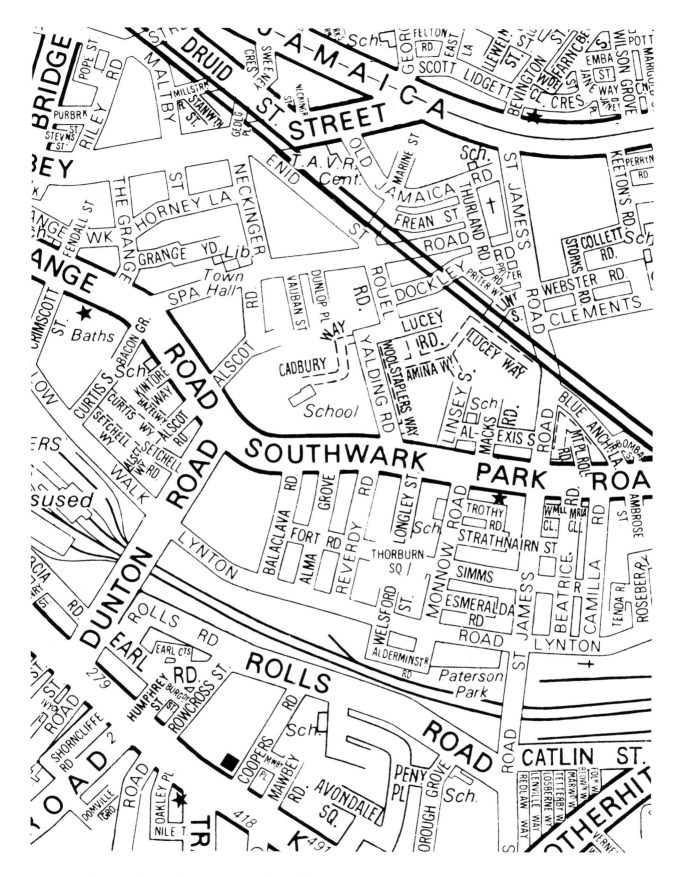

Bethnal Green and Mile End Old Town

As with all of today's East End there are very few similarities or continuities apparent here between the 1740s and the 1980s. Take, for instance, Bethnal Green, parts of which are shown at the top of Rocque's map: not only was its population only a fraction of its present total but it was then quite clearly separate from London. In June 1663 Samuel Pepys had visited his friend Sir William Rider at Kirby Hall – one of the buildings just below the Watch House (2/5) – and remarked in his *Diary* on 'the greatest Quantity of Strawberrys I ever saw, and good'. Pepys later returned here in September 1666 during the Great Fire in order to store his valuables, amongst them his *Diary*; he recounts how he drove up Dog Row (5/5), our Cambridge Heath Road, on a cart at 4 o'clock in the morning clad only in his nightgown.

Up to Rocque's period Bethnal Green had always been a fashionable place in which to live. The Bishops of London owned a country mansion just off the north-east corner of this section, near our Victoria Park. The Green itself (3/6) had been purchased off Lady Wentworth, the local landowner, by nearby residents in 1690, and a guide book of 1754 informed readers that 'this Parish hath the Face of a Country, affording every Thing to render it pleasant, Fields, Pasturage-grounds for Cattle, and formerly Woods and Marshes.' But slowly London was creeping nearer Bethnal Green, filling up the fields with cheap housing and gloomy little alleys.

In the early nineteenth century Bethnal Green was indeed swallowed up by the metropolis, becoming one of its poorest districts. In his *Oliver Twist* of 1839, Charles Dickens describes Fagin walking from Spitalfields to Bill Sykes' den in Bethnal Green:

He kept on his course, though many winding and narrow ways, until he reached Bethnal Green; then, turning suddenly off to the left, he soon became involved in a maze of the mean and dirty streets which abound in that close and densely-populated quarter.

Clearly much was changed since Rocque's survey.

Drift Way (1/7) became Roman Road – despite this name it was in fact Old Ford Road just off the top of the map which had been used by the Roman legions marching to Colchester and East Anglia – and the tree-lined track (4/8) running down from the north is now Globe Road. The Red Cow Lane (8/9) branching off Dog Row is Cleveland Way – the Wentworths were also the earls of Cleveland.

The Mile End Old Town lining what is our Whitechapel Road and Mile End Road had grown up because of the highway's volume of traffic, not just a route for drovers but also, as Defoe observed in his novel *Roxana* of 1724, used by the gentry riding out of the crowded City to take the country air. Ominously enough Rocque shows the actual Ducking Pond (9/3) which tested the innocence or otherwise of suspected witches. Ducking Pond Lane is now Brady Street and Ducking Pond Row is Durward Street.

On the other side of the road is an empty rectangular patch of ground (10/2) which was soon to be the London Hospital. This institution had begun as the London Infirmary in Moorfields in 1740, moving to Prestcot Street, Whitechapel because the original premises had proved inadequate. Again too small, the hospital's governors decided to purchase a site well out in the country and settled on Mile End Old Town. Two obvious drawbacks to this location were dismissed, the first being that the road outside had an open sewer running down the middle and the second that Chapel Mount (10/1), once fortified by the Parliamentary forces during the Civil War of the 1640s, was now a huge rubbish dump. The foundation stone of the new hospital was laid in 1752 and it started to admit patients five years later.

Returning to the north side of Mile End Old Town, on the east corner with Dog Row had stood in 1665 the district's plague pit. Stepney then had suffered particularly badly, losing over 6,500 people and prompting the statesman Lord Clarendon to fear for the safety of the Navy – traditionally many sailors had been recruited from this neighbourhood. Sir

Christopher Wren's Trinity Almshouses (9/5), with the chapel at the end, have survived to this day. Built in 1695 on land given by a Captain Henry Mudd, these almshouses of the Trinity Brethren were intended for 'twenty-eight decayed masters and commanders of ships, or the widows of such'. In the late nineteenth century attempts were made to pull them down, but a campaign led by William Morris and others – one of Morris's last interventions before his death in 1896 – ensured their preservation. Bombed during the 2nd World War the Trinity Almshouses were carefully restored.

Mile End Old Town was in the 1740s a rather smart part of London. The 1754 edition of John Stow's *Survey of London* referred to earlier described it as 'built with many good Houses, inhabited by divers Sea Captains and Commanders of Ships, and other Persons of good Quality'. A few years after this was published, in a little strip of housing called Assembly Row which was to be on the south side of the road opposite Camel Row (8/6), a certain Captain James Cook moved into no.7 in 1764 (it is now 88 Mile End Road and bears a commemorative plaque). Cook lived here for the rest of his shore-based life, leaving in 1776 for what turned out to be his final voyage. He had once worked on the Newcastle-London coal run before joining the Royal Navy in 1755, signing up at a riverside tavern in Wapping. When in 1774 he was asked by natives where his home was, Cook replied 'Stepney'. After his death his widow continued to live on at no.7 Assembly Row for some years.

Rocque's map of Mile End Old Town shows little business activity other than 'Westfield's Brew house' (7/7), the forerunner of the breweries which now fringe the Mile End Road. There is a bowling green (11/4) but otherwise the area is farmland. However the wide open spaces had always offered a convenient rallying place for large numbers of people. In 1381 the boy king Richard II had confronted Wat Tyler's peasants here. Richard pledged to draw up the charters which would have ended feudalism in this country, but later reneged on his promise.

Soon after Rocque's survey, the name Stepney began to replace that of Mile End. Some of the houses now looking out onto our Stepney Green Gardens actually pre-date Rocque: no.37, for example, was built in the 1690s. The '13 Houses' (9/8) shown on Rocque's map would certainly have been inhabited by wealthy families, enjoying the rural setting but with the knowledge that the City was only a short distance to the west. During the Victorian era however, Stepney became industrialised, overcrowded and poor. In 1730 the population of the whole of East London was approximately 120,000. When the Metropolitan Borough of Stepney was formed in 1900 its population alone was in the region of 300,000.

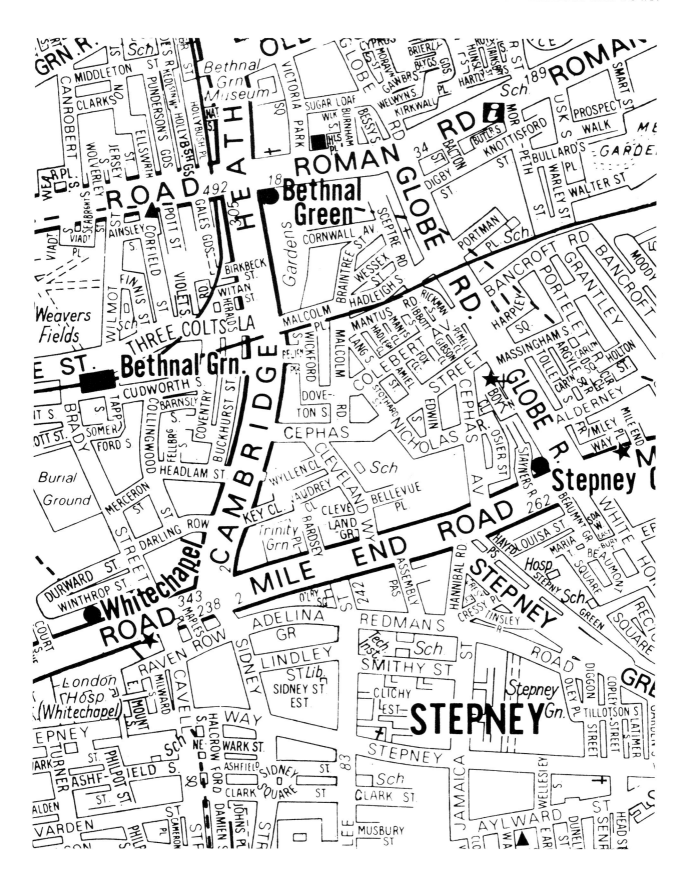

Reproduced by permission of Geographers' A-Z Map Co Ltd.

Wapping and Rotherhithe

John Rocque's map of this area underlines the fact that the East London of the eighteenth century was very largely a creation of the riverside, its trades and occupations dependent upon its maritime links. In 1754 Henry Fielding boarded a ship to Lisbon here on what turned out to be his last voyage; he recorded in his *Journal*

we then lay, in the confines of Wapping and Rotherhithe, tasting a delicious mixture of the air of both these sweet places, and enjoying the concord of sweet sounds of seamen, watermen, fish-women, oyster-women, and of all the vociferous inhabitants of both shores . . .

– one suspects that his use of the word 'sweet' was heavily ironical.

What we call Shadwell was in Rocque's day still open countryside. Bluegate Field (4/2), which in the nineteenth century was renowned as one of the most squalid parts of the metropolis, then looked out onto fields. Today our Commercial Road thunders along at the top of the section, but in the 1740s it was just an anonymous track. Sun Tavern Fields (5/6) was where ships' ropes and cables were made, eventually giving rise to the name of Cable Street. Ominous, as a foretaste of things to come, is Cutthroat Lane just to the east. The only building to the north of Ratcliff Highway which is still identifiable today is the church of St. George in the East (5/1), yet another creation of the 50 New Churches Act and built by Wren's former colleague Nicholas Hawksmoor. Constructed of Portland stone, it was completed in 1726 and its 160ft. tower was and still is visible from all over the neighbourhood. After bombing in the 1940s, a new church was constructed actually inside the exterior of Hawksmoor's building. The churchyard is now a pleasant recreation ground. Cannon Street (5/1) to its west was so named because the Parliamentary forces in the Civil War of the 1640s had put up a fort nearby.

Apart from the numerous sugar refineries close to St. George's, which were often run by German immigrants and led to the district sometimes being called 'Little Germany', the Ratcliff Highway was a sailors' haunt. Just like Wapping High Street it was full of taverns, brothels, dancing-rooms and opium dens and had acquired a similarly notorious reputation. More bizarrely the Highway also specialised in the sale of wild animals: for instance, there was Mr. Charles Jamrach 'naturalist' of nos.179-180 who dealt with elephants, giraffes, lions and monkeys – the business closed down during the 1st World War when the firm was unable to obtain further supplies of animals. Further east, just off Upper Shadwell, was the church of St. Paul (6/6) – the land had once belonged to the Dean and Chapter of St. Paul's Cathedral – which was more familiarly known as 'the Church of Sea Captains'. Captain James Cook was a parishioner in the eighteenth century and had his eldest son baptised here. In 1790 the ageing John Wesley preached what turned out to be his last sermon at St. Paul's, having been at Christ Church, Spitalfields in the morning. Although first built in 1669 the church we see today was reconstructed in 1820 after the Napoleonic wars as a 'Waterloo' church, an expression of gratitude for the Duke of Wellington's victory over Napoleon Bonaparte.

Looking down towards Wapping, Rocque shows the infamous Execution Dock Stairs (11/3), the spot where pirates were put to death and their corpses left hanging as a deterrent to other potential wrongdoers. When Captain Kidd was hanged here in March 1701 the execution was bungled and Kidd could easily have escaped but proved too drunk to seize his opportunity.

On either side were more sailors' lodgings and places of entertainment, not a district in which the pedestrian lingered. In 1698 Ned Ward recorded just what he saw here:

Sometimes we met in the streeet with a boat's crew, just come on shore in search of those land debaucheries which the sea denies 'em, looking such wild, staring, gruesome, uncouth animals, that a litter of squab rhinoceroses, dressed up in human apparel, could not have made a more ungainly appearance. They were so mercurial in their actions, and rude in their behaviour, that a woman could not pass by 'em without a sense of shame or fear of danger.

Ironically enough some of these riverside Wapping haunts – pubs like the Prospect of Whitby which claims to have been founded in 1520 or the Town of Ramsgate – are now haunted instead by tourists.

Despite extensive German bombing, the modern map shows that the maze of streets surveyed by Rocque has persisted to this day, even if several have new names: Old Gravel Lane (8/2) is Wapping Lane and New Gravel Lane (7/4) is our Garnet Street. The major change has come further eastwards with the opening of the King Edward VII Memorial Park (or Shadwell Park) in 1922 on the site of what had been Shadwell Fish Market – Rocque shows the first market buildings (6/7).

In both the eighteenth and the nineteenth centuries Wapping and Rotherhithe possessed a rather murky aura, and in 1843 the Brunels' Thames Tunnel joined them together. From the time when he was appointed Chief Engineer at the age of only 21, Isambard Kingdom Brunel threw himself into the task of constructing the first ever tunnel under a major river. Although a project which took far longer than anticipated, the Thames Tunnel was completed in 1843 after 18 years' work and at a cost of over £600,000. It was opened by Queen Victoria who was prevailed upon to walk through it. However the road approaches to the tunnel were never built and after an initial burst of popularity it became a favoured spot for prostitutes and pickpockets. Never used by road traffic as intended it is now part of the East London line of the Metropolitan Underground service.

Like Wapping, Rotherhithe was also in Rocque's time a riverside village, centred around the parish church of St. Mary (13/5). Wharves and warehouses lined Redriff Street but only a few hundred yards away were the fields and market gardens which survived until devoured by the growth of Victorian Rotherhithe: in 1801 its population was less than 10,000 but a century later it was four times that figure. However St. Mary's has survived as a fine example of a Georgian church. Its predecessor on this site had gradually rotted away as a result of the frequent floods experienced by Rotherhithe and it was rebuilt in 1715: the visitor now walks up steps to get inside, where the four pillars were once ships' masts.

Opposite St. Mary was a school, founded in 1613 'for the education of eight sons of seamen, with a salary of three pounds per annum for the master'. From 1742 it was a charity school and outside are the figures of a boy and a girl in appropriate eighteenth-century costume. Just beside Church Stairs (13/6) was and is the Mayflower public house, its name indicating that this was the spot from which the Mayflower set out on its journey to North America in 1620. The captain of the ship, Christopher Jones, was buried in the churchyard and there is a memorial to him inside St. Mary's. Close to Prince's Stairs (13/3) is another old pub which would have been known to Rocque called the Angel inn, an old smugglers' den. Pepys had been a visitor and so it is thought was the cruel Judge Jeffreys who came here to enjoy a drink whilst observing the pirates' corpses hanging directly opposite at Execution Dock.

The major changes in this section of Rocque's map came with the construction of the Surrey Dock, dealt with later on. Brunel Road in which the Rotherhithe underground station stands, is of course a tribute to the Brunels father and son.

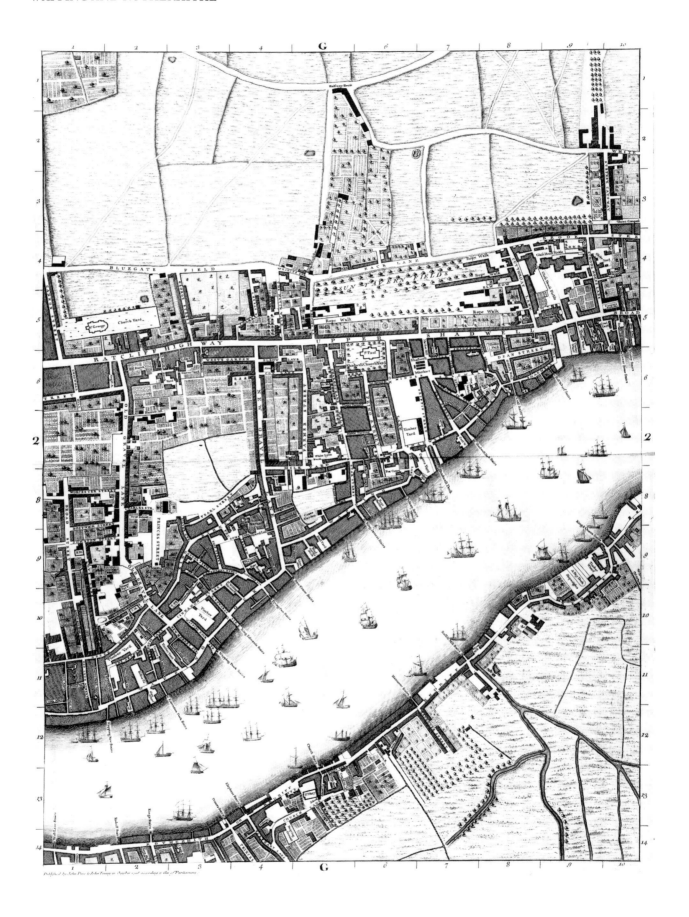

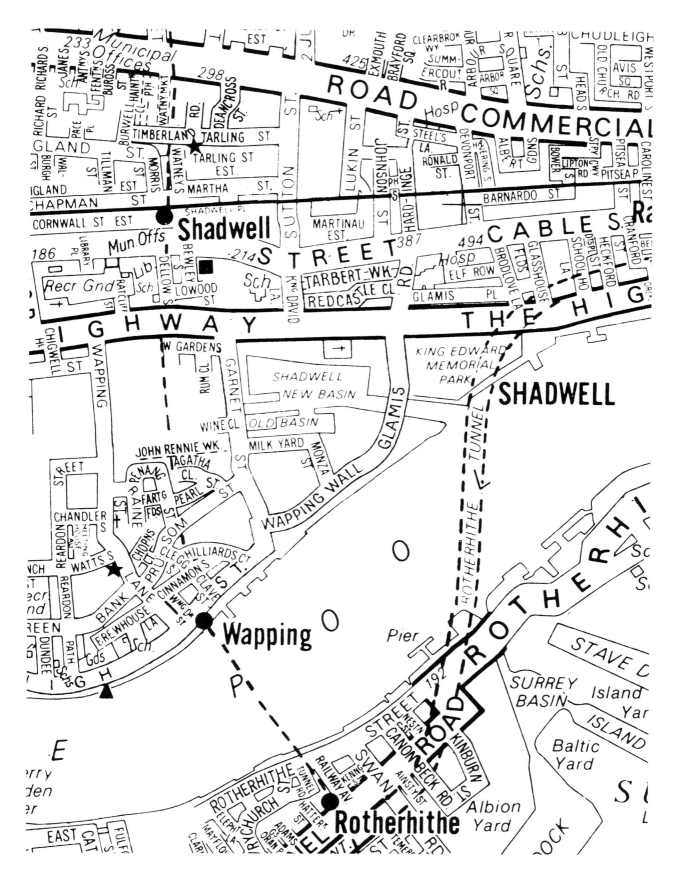

Reproduced by permission of Geographers' A-Z Map Co Ltd.

Rotherhithe and Southwark Park

The main feature of this section of Rocque's map is not in fact a part of London at all but instead is the dedication to the Lord Mayor and Aldermen. As explained earlier, the patronage of the City Corporation would have been vital to Rocque and Pine in obtaining subscriptions for the future publication of their map. It is notable that the inscription is signed by John Pine and John Tinney but not by John Rocque. Of the cherubs displayed within the fancy scrollwork, they all hold items or commodities connected with the burgeoning wealth of the City. On the pole of the central cherub hangs the Cap of Liberty.

The Lord Mayor Sir Richard Hoare was a member of the banking family which had been founded by his grandfather Richard Hoare. He had begun as a goldsmith in Fleet Street but then expanded into banking, setting up at no.37 under the sign of the Golden Bottle – a symbol which still hangs there. Samuel Pepys was one of his customers, and Pepys left him a ring in his will. Our Sir Richard Hoare was elected Lord Mayor in 1745. Of the Aldermen, the most distinguished was Sir John Barnard, wine merchant and politician. He was MP for the City of London from 1722 until 1761, being an opponent of Sir Robert Walpole who generously acknowledged that he had frequently felt the power of Sir John Barnard's speeches. Barnard was also an implacable enemy of the stage.

Above the dedication the map shows the district now probably best described as South Bermondsey and Rotherhithe. At first sight there seem to be few continuities between the 1740s and the 1980s, but Rocque's Road to Deptford is our Lower Road and the anonymous and twisted passage on the left is now Southwark Park Road. The land between them is today's Southwark Park which was opened in the late 1860s and covers 65 acres.

The rural splendour of Bermondsey meant that for centuries it had been fashionable to own a country residence here: in the top left-hand corner can be seen New and Old Paradise Streets (1/2), and the word 'Paradise' actually derives from words meaning 'closed garden'. In the early fifteenth century King Henry IV used to come here when he periodically suffered from leprosy. He stayed in an old stone mansion, being treated by the Prior of Bermondsey 'who was eminent for his skill in physic'.

In Rocque's day the area still maintained its reputation as one of the healthiest places in London: Lysons in his *Environs of London* (1810) commented that

The disproportion of the burials to the births seems to denote a healthy spot, and indeed Rotherhithe has been remarked for the salubrity of its air, and the infrequency of infectious disorders there; a circumstance which has been accounted for from the flux and reflux of the tides passing through the common sewers.

The fields and gardens depicted by Rocque played an important part in supplying the capital with food – it was a reciprocal process as the horse manure resulting from the thousands of these animals parading the metropolis was put to good use here. John Gerard in his *Herball* published in 1597 had written of the melons which he had found in the vicinity, and in Rocque's day the district was well-known for the high quality of its strawberries and figs.

Apart from its fruit and vegetables there was also soon to be a pleasure garden called the St. Helena Tea Gardens just off the Road to Deptford – underneath the middle of the dedication – which was opened in 1770 and covered 5½ acres. It has been described by Mary Boast in *The Story of Rotherhithe*:

Here fashionable people, even the Prince Regent, the future King George IV, came to enjoy music and dancing. Later, in the days of Queen Victoria, the gardens became very popular with ordinary people as there were all kinds of entertainments, concerts, sports, fireworks, tight-rope walkers, performing dogs and a special attraction, 'the centrifugal railway'. The gardens closed in 1881 and were built over.[10]

Lord Mayor's Show of 1761: the procession travelling along Cheapside with attendant noise, bustle and fights: King George III and the royal family are watching from a balcony on the left: St. Mary-le-Bow stands directly opposite.

All we are left with is the name St. Helena Road.

The portion of the map to the east of the Road to Deptford was transformed in Victorian times by the construction of the Surrey Docks. These docks specialised in the handling of timber imported from Scandinavia, which explains the existence of the Swedish church today on Lower Road and also the Norwegian and Finnish churches by Albion Road. At the top of the spire of the Norwegian church sits a Viking ship, and the signs on the public lavatories outside are in both English and Norwegian. The church is dedicated to St. Olaf – there is a statue of him just inside the building – who had helped the English defeat the Danes at the Battle of London Bridge in 1014. Several Norse sagas told how Olaf commanded his men to pull down London Bridge and thus destroy the Danish forces commanding the bridge; one of the sagas ends:

> London bridge is broke down,
> Gold is won and bright renown,
> Shields resounding,

> War-horns sounding,
> Hildar shouting in the din!
> Arrows singing,
> Mailcoats ringing –
> Odin makes our Olaf win.

Near to the entrance of the Norwegian church is Rotherhithe Tunnel, opened in 1908 in order to relieve London Bridge and Tower Bridge from some of the weight of traffic. Bermondsey itself had grown from a population of 17,000 in 1801 to more than four times this by 1881. Over the entrance to the approach road is a part of the tunnelling shield used in its construction.

The names of the modern roads generally have associations with people or places of local importance. Jamaica Road is called after the old Jamaica House which stood nearby and itself is thought to have been a tribute to the birthplace of rum. Gomm Road which bisects Southwark Park is called after the general and Constable of the Tower Sir William Gomm: he was first commissioned into the army aged 10 and died at age 90 after 80 years continuous service – a record unlikely to be beaten. Culling was another of the Gomm family names. Galleywall on the left of the modern map, according to Sheila Fairfield, approached 'a place called the Gallow Wall in a record of the reign of Henry VII (1485-1509)'.[11]

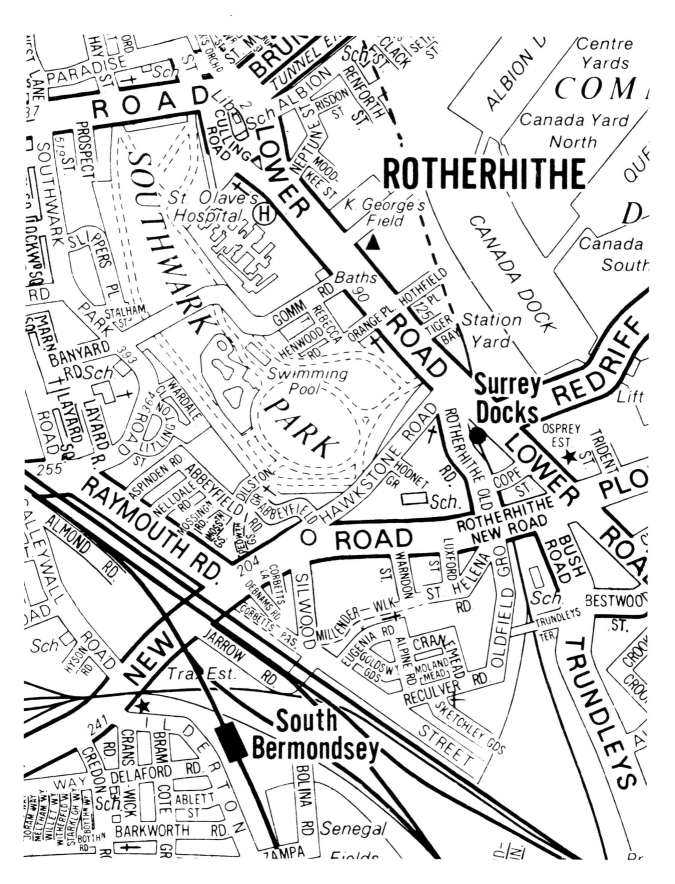

Reproduced by permission of Geographers' A-Z Map Co Ltd.

Stepney and Bow

Of all the parts of London surveyed by John Rocque 250 years ago, this was perhaps the least populated. Leaving aside the village clustered around the church of St. Dunstan's and a few dwellings on either side of Mile End Old Town, the map emphasises the rural character and setting of old Stepney – the Stepney of which Thomas More wrote to a friend in 1504 that 'Here you find nothing but bounteous gifts of nature and the saint-like tokens of innocence.' In the Domesday Book of 1086 Stepney's population was estimated at about 700 people, and in the intervening seven centuries there had been little expansion. In Defoe's *Moll Flanders*, published in 1722, Moll tells of how 'I walked frequently out into the villages round the town, to see if nothing would fall in my way there'; from a house in Stepney she managed to steal two rings.

Lying some miles from London, Stepney was much used as a convenient burial ground and Rocque shows two Jewish cemeteries to the north of Mile End Old Town. The 'old' burying ground (6/1) is now behind Albert Stern House at no.253 Mile End Road, and one can see the various graves either by application or by peering over the wall at its side. This was the cemetery of those Spanish and Portuguese Jews who had fled from the terrors of the Inquisition, establishing their own congregation in the City of London in 1656, the first since all Jewish people had been expelled from England by Edward I in 1290. A few years after Rocque's survey, in 1790, a hospital and a home for the elderly were added to the burial ground.

The 'new' burying ground (5/3) is today somewhat overshadowed by extensions to the institution which now occupies the site of Bancroft's Hospital (6/2): Queen Mary College. A former Lord Mayor of London of the early eighteenth century, Bancroft had left £28,000 in his will to the Drapers' Company for the building of almshouses, a chapel and a school. In the nineteenth century the Drapers' Company joined forces with the trustees of the New Philosophic Institute, a merger which resulted in the People's

Palace of 1887. Out of this grew the East London Technical College which in turn became Queen Mary College in 1934. The College later took over the Queen's Hall which had provided concerts and lectures up to the 1940s.

The Essex Road leading to the east is now our Bow Road, but in the 1740s it was still the main highway for travellers journeying to Essex and East Anglia. The stone bridge over the River Lea had been built in the twelfth century on bow-shaped arches, thus giving its name to the neighbouring village. In Rocque's day Bow was on the outskirts of London and even in the early nineteenth century its population was less than 3,000; by the Edwardian period however it was nearly 50,000 and Bow was very securely a part of the capital.

In his *London Spy* of 1698 Ned Ward describes a coach journey from Stratford to Whitechapel along the Essex Road and Mile End Old Town, a passage which brings out the discomforts faced by all travellers in Rocque's England:

Our Stratford tub, by the assistance of its carrionly tits of different colours, outran the smoothness of the road and enter'd upon London's cobble stones with as frightful a rumbling as an empty haycart. It had no more sway than a funeral hearse, or a country wagon, so that we were jumbled about like so many peas in a child's rattle, running a great hazard of dislocation at every kennel jolt. This we endured till we were brought within Whitechapel Bars, where we lighted from our stubborn caravan, with our elbows and shoulders as black and blue as a rural Joan that has been under the pinches of an angry fairy.

Of the few roads shown by Rocque all have survived. The Road to Bow, for instance, is in part Bow Common and the Foot Path to Bow is our Hamlets Way. The derivation of Rhodeswell Road is also clear: Rocque shows the Rhode's Well (9/7). Wholly new since the 1740s are Grove Road which runs down from the north and also Burdett Road, named after the Victorian philanthropist Angela Burdett Coutts in 1862. This was built in order to link up the riverside areas with

Victoria Park, opened in the 1840s. Regent's Canal – or as it is called today, the Grand Union Canal – was also constructed after Rocque's day.

In the bottom left-hand corner of Rocque's map is the ancient church of St. Dunstan's (12/2), founded by and named after the powerful Archbishop Dunstan of the tenth century. The buildings which both Rocque surveyed and we see today are largely the creation of the fifteenth century. Although some of the churchyard has been sliced away in the last two centuries it still manages to convey the country atmosphere of old Stepney. Few buildings lay then between St. Dunstan's and the Thames, thus accounting for its name as 'the Church of the High Seas'. Traditionally any child buried at sea was a parishioner of this church. The churchyard was famous in the eighteenth century for some of the inscriptions on the gravestones, such as:

> Here lies the body of Daniel Saull,
> Spittle-fields weaver, and that's all.

The highwayman Jack Sheppard was christened in this church.

To the south of St. Dunstan's churchyard can just be seen the Mercers' Almshouses (13/2). Rebuilt in 1856 they are now called the Dame Jane Mico Almshouses. The anonymous road passing by them is White Horse Road, whilst Rocque's Ocean Street (10/1) has given its name to the Ocean Housing Estate. But fundamentally Rocque's map underlines the fact that the 'East End' was a product of nineteenth-century industrialisation and a marked growth in population. Until then Mile End Old Town, Bow and Stepney were indeed little more than the Tower of London's hamlets.

In the Victorian period, the fields of Stepney were submerged under a mass of bricks and mortar, often developments carried out by the local landowners. For instance Simon Jenkins has noted that:

The Mercers Company, holders of substantial lands in the old Manor Stepney, put up as many as 1,100 houses for tradespeople and artisans covering ninety acres of Stepney in the years between 1811 and 1851.

Despite heavy bombing during the 2nd World War – a third of the borough's housing was destroyed – several streets survived untouched. Something of an oddity was Lord Tredegar's Tredegar Square which stands to the north of Mile End Road and whose grandiose houses seem quite out of place.

The expansion of the population resulted eventually in an increase in the number of deaths in the district. One eighteenth-century graveyard was that of Globe Fields just off the north-west corner of this map, and where, according to Denis Keeling, corpses were dug up after a few years in order to make room for new arrivals, the coffins being burnt on the sexton's fire; the burial service was conducted by bogus clergymen; and gravediggers were given large doses of spirits. The City of London and Tower Hamlets Cemetery, visible on the right-hand side of the modern map, was opened in 1841. Looking at the inscriptions of the gravestones today, it is clear that seafaring occupations outnumber all the others put together – as is appropriate in view of St. Dunstan's traditions:

The most common description is 'mariner' or 'master mariner' and according to the inscriptions a great many of them were buried not at Tower Hamlets, but at sea.[13]

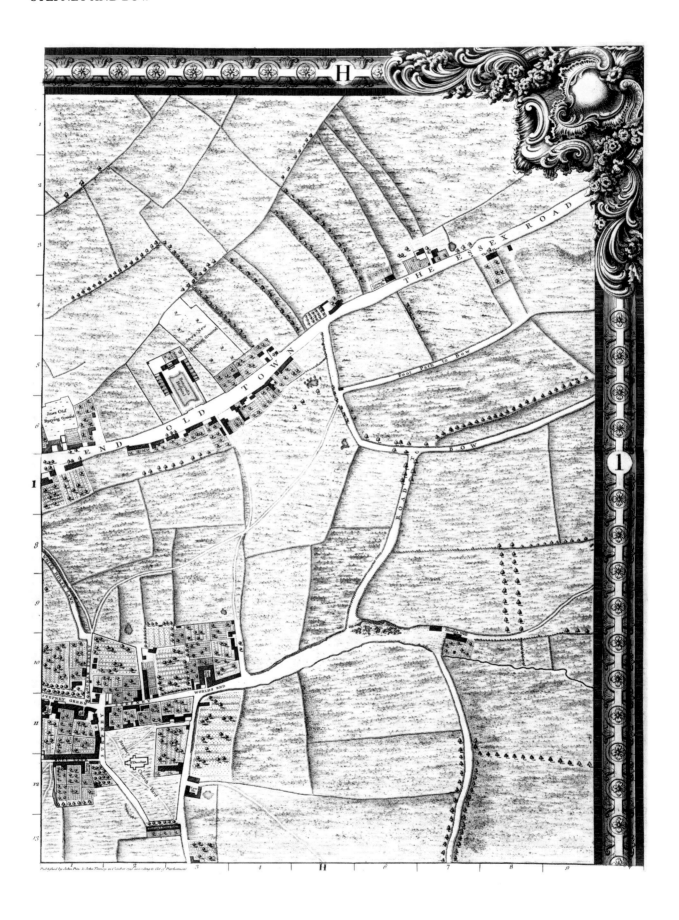

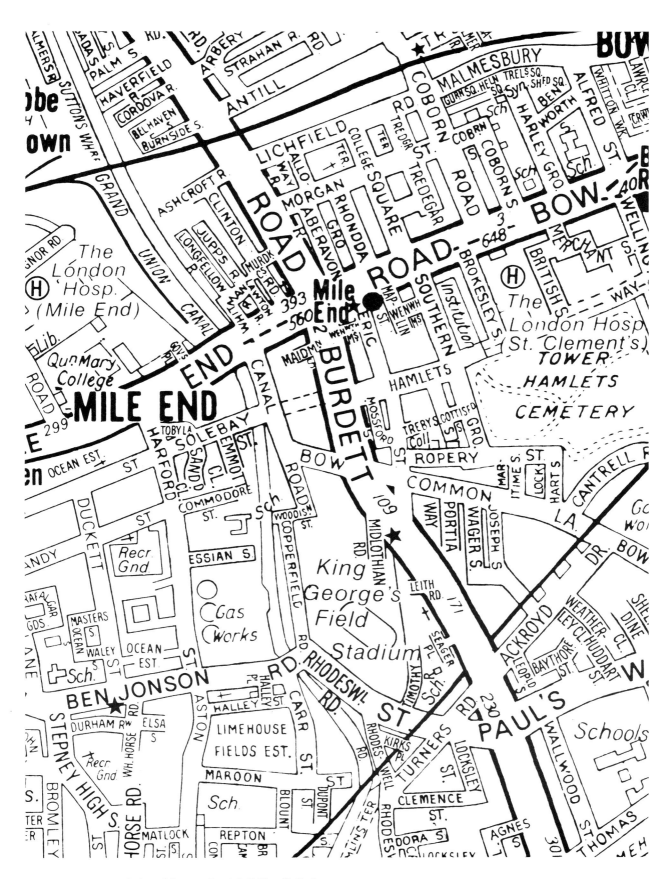

Reproduced by permission of Geographers' A-Z Map Co Ltd.

Limehouse and Rotherhithe

Rocque's map yet again shows how rural our 'East End' and 'South London' were in the middle of the eighteenth century, the only development being the dwellings and shipwrights' yards clustered together on the riverside. The maritime associations of this district had always been foremost: Rotherhithe or Redriff as it was still generally called in Rocque's day, derived from the Saxon words 'redhra' meaning a sailor and 'hyth' a port or haven. Ratcliff Cross (5/2) for example on the north bank had been the point from which Tudor and Elizabethan seafarers departed to the unknown – today a stone in Shadwell Park commemorates their names – and Sir Walter Raleigh had lived in the neighbourhood whilst organising his Cadiz expedition in 1596.

Many seamen were also recruited from this area, although as Samuel Pepys recorded in June 1667 of a Dutch raid up the Thames, financial considerations were paramount:

> several seamen came this morning to me to tell me that if I would get their tickets paid, they would go and do all they could against the Dutch; but otherwise they would not venture being killed and lose all they have already fought for – so that I was forced to try what I could do to get them paid. And endeed, the hearts as well as affections of the seamen are turned away; and in the open streets of Wapping, and up and down, the wifes have cried publicly, 'This comes of your not paying our husbands; and now your work is undone, or done by hands that understand it not'.

Just above Ratcliff Cross lies Butcher Row (4/2), a street occupied as the name suggests by meat dealers, often German, who were unable to gain admission to the City guild. Today the Royal Foundation of St. Katharine is located here. Founded near the Tower of London in 1147 by Queen Matilda, the Foundation was both a hospital and a sanctuary. When the docks of the same name were constructed in the 1820s the Foundation moved to Regent's Park and then Poplar before coming here after the 2nd World War. The Master's House was once the vicarage of the church of St. James, Ratcliff, which had been built in 1837 in order to minister to the expanding population but was destroyed by German bombing.

To the east of Ratcliff is Limehouse, once the site of several limekilns. Rocque depicts a 'Lime-Kiln Dock' and a 'Lime-Kiln Yard' (7/8). Despite this noxious activity, however, Limehouse in the seventeenth and eighteenth centuries was a fashionable place in which to live. The ubiquitous Samuel Pepys once came here in October 1661 along with other dignitaries for a meal with Captain Marsh. His house 'hath been their ancestors for this 250 years', but Pepys did not entirely enjoy his evening:

> We had a very good and handsome dinner, and excellent wine. I not being neat in clothes, which I find a great fault in me, could not be so merry as otherwise and at all times I am and can be, when I am in good habitt . . .

Of the Limehouse surveyed by Rocque, a number of features still remain. Narrow Street (5/3) has retained its long and straggly characteristics, whilst the houses at 82-86 date back to the 1730s. The Grapes public house possesses a Victorian front but would certainly have been known to Rocque. Sermon Lane (1/5) at the top is now our Salmon Lane: its original name is explained by its use by the people of Limehouse on their way to St. Dunstan's on Stepney Green. By the early eighteenth century the growth of the local population warranted their having their own church, and so Nicholas Hawksmoor built the third of his three East London churches carried out under the provisions of the 50 New Churches Act of 1711. Consecrated in 1730, Hawksmoor's St. Ann's (3/9) dominated the skyline and to a large extent still does – the church is supposed to boast the highest church clock in London. Three Colt Street still runs to the east of the churchyard.

The then insignificant Rose Lane (3/5) was to become Commercial Road, the busy highway opened by the dock companies in 1810 in order to ferry their goods into the City of London. Everyone else had to pay up at the tollgates. Our Limehouse Basin and Limehouse Cut were completed in 1770, some twenty-five years after the publication of Rocque's map, enabling barges to use the River Lea without having to make the arduous journey right around the Isle of Dogs. The Basin and the Cut were symptomatic of the accelerating industrialisation of the district, prompting those who could afford it to move out of Limehouse in the course of the Victorian period – the railway to Essex opened in 1860. Limehouse Hole (8/9) was also to be notorious, the place where Charles Dickens put Rogue Riderhood in *Our Mutual Friend*:

Rogue Riderhood dwelt deep and dark in Limehouse Hole, among the riggers, and the mast, oar and block makers, and the boat-builders, and the sail-lofts . . . It was a wretched little shop, with a roof that any man standing in it could touch with his hand; little better than cellar or cave, down three steps.

Limehouse is as far east as Rocque's survey took him; he would have continued into Poplar and the Isle of Dogs, both districts which were spacious and largely unpopulated until the nineteenth century. However, Daniel Defoe noted in the 1720s that the postal system from here was highly efficient:

you may send a letter from Ratcliff or Limehouse in the East, to the farthest part of Westminster for a penny, and that several times in the same day.

Over on the other bank of the Thames, the main part of Rotherhithe was centred around the church of St. Mary further to the west. Here the various roads – today all subsumed under the name of Rotherhithe Street, one of the longest roads in London – offered a route to and from the shipwrights' and timber yards as well as the storehouses: Mrs. Peachum in *The Beggar's Opera* of 1728 refers to 'our warehouses at Redriff

among the seamen'. As for the Rotherhithe shipwrights, in 1612 a Royal Charter was granted to 'the Master, Wardens and Commonalty of the Art or Mystery of Shipwrights of Redrith' in respect of their 'ships, carvels, hoys, pinnacles, ketches, lighters, boats, barges and wherries'. But not even this charter could prevent the periodic slumps which hit this district; the 1754 edition of Stow's *Survey of London* says of Rotherhithe that 'This Parish consists of Abundance of Seafaring Men's Families; which increaseth the Poor there exceedingly.'

One attractive building which Rocque would have surveyed does still remain, the Nelson Dock House built in about 1740. It stands in what was then Queen Street (11/6). That nothing else remains, demonstrates the wholesale transformation effected by the construction of the Surrey Docks in the nineteenth century, its 136 acres tearing up the fields shown by Rocque. Badly bombed in the 2nd World War and then closed down in 1970, recent developments are, ironically enough, returning it to the state of Rocque's gardens and trees: a Nature Park has just been started near Lavender Dock.

As the Thames arches around Rotherhithe both the modern map and Rocque's show Cuckold's Point (10/7). The origin of this name goes back to the reign of King John when the king himself was out hunting one day in Charlton and came across a miller's pretty wife. John and his new girlfriend were surprised by the sudden return home of the miller who demanded compensation for what he regarded as damage to his chattels. The king awarded him as much land as he could see, which to the west of Charlton stretched to Rotherhithe, and also the right to hold an annual fair on the day in question, October 18th. A pole with a pair of horns on top stood at Cuckold's Point up to the nineteenth century.

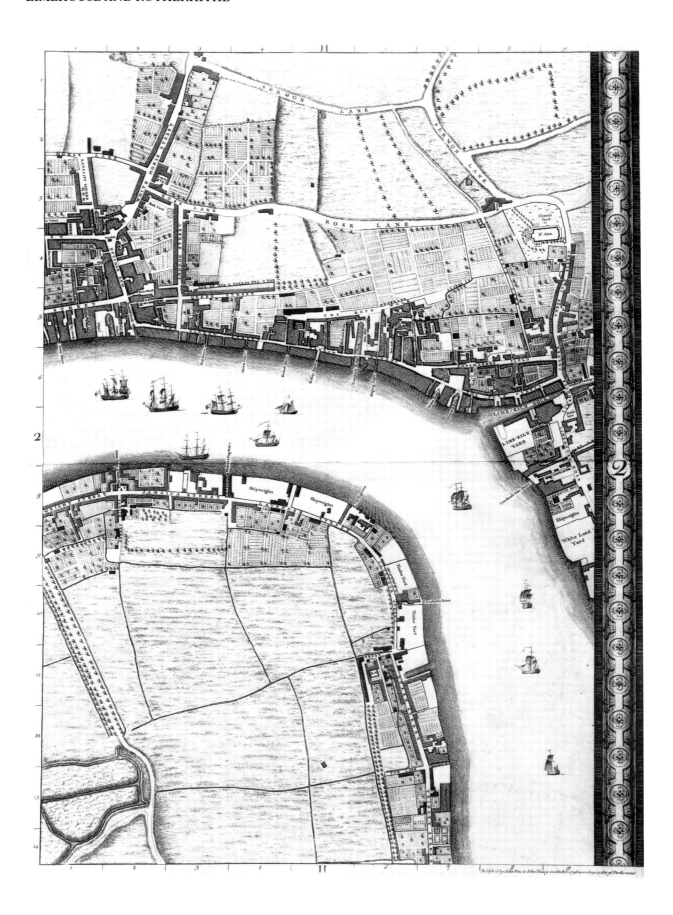

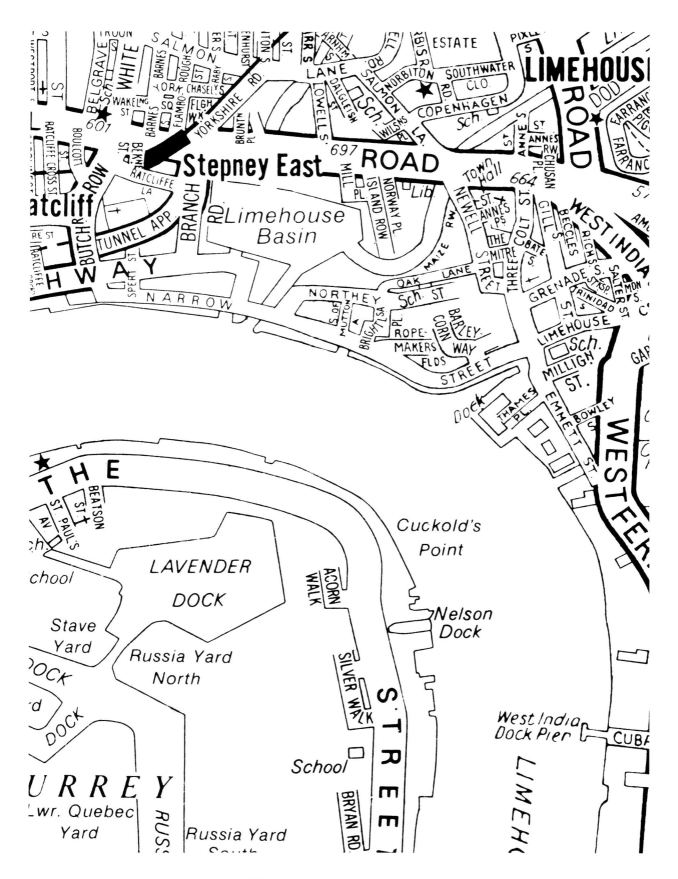

Rotherhithe and Deptford

Yet again another section of Rocque's map of London shows an area which is barely inhabited, at least by our standards. But to Daniel Defoe, writing of Deptford in his *A Tour Through The Whole Island of Great Britain* published little more than a decade before Rocque began his survey,

this town was formerly reckoned, at least two miles off from Redriff, and that over the marshes too, a place unlikely ever to be inhabited; and yet now, by the increase of buildings in that town itself, and the many streets erected at Redriff, and by the docks and building-yards on the riverside, which stand between both, the town of Deptford, and the streets of Redriff, or Rotherhithe (as they write it) are effactually joined, and the buildings daily increasing . . .

If only Defoe could see Deptford today.

This section is dominated by the Upper Wet Dock (6/5) in the centre. The land here had formerly been owned by a Mr. John Howland, but as part of the marriage settlement for his daughter Elizabeth it was transferred to a Russell, one of the family who had developed Covent Garden. The bridegroom's father, the then Duke of Bedford, thereupon built London's first enclosed dock, calling it the Howland Dock. A fine mansion (6/3) was positioned at its west end and a barrier of trees planted on both sides in order to shield docked vessels from the wind.

Before the Howland Dock was opened in 1700 ships had tied up in the Thames, prey to the elements. Very soon afterwards, in November 1703, the efficacy of the dock was confirmed when a storm destroyed the ships out in the river but damaged only slightly one of the sheltered vessels. Although Rocque shows only six ships at berth, the dock could hold 120 at any one time. For much of the eighteenth century it specialised in the whaling trade and was often called the Greenland Dock. In the Victorian period it handled timber and grain, and is now in part a watersports centre.

This part of London had always maintained strong maritime links, from as early as the fourteenth century when in Edward III's reign a fleet against the French had been fitted out here by the Black Prince and John of Gaunt. The King's Yard (13/6), or as it was sometimes called Deptford Dockyard, had been founded in 1513 by Henry VIII, a date often regarded as marking the establishment of the Royal Navy. In all, the yard covered some 30 acres. A few years later Henry's daughter Elizabeth commanded Francis Drake and his ship *The Golden Hind* to put in here in 1581. A banquet was held on board – a contemporary chronicler records that the Queen 'consecrated it with great ceremonie, pompe, and magnificence eternally to be remembered' – after which she knighted Drake. When *The Golden Hind* was removed from active service she was stored just off the riverside as an important reminder of England's nautical prowess; she finally disintegrated over the years.

The King's Yard was still much in use throughout the eighteenth century, as Henry Fielding noted in his *Journal of a Voyage to Lisbon* for 1754 when he sailed past on his way to Portugal:

The yards of Deptford and of Woolwich are noble sights, and give us a just idea of the great perfection to which we are arrived in building those floating castles, and the figure which we may always make in Europe among the other maritime powers.

However in the Victorian period the transition from wooden ships to ironclads meant that the yards of Woolwich prevailed over those at Deptford which were handicapped by having shallower water: the King's Yard closed down in 1896.

The Victualling Yard (11/7) had been under the control of Samuel Pepys when he was appointed Surveyor General of the Victualling Department in 1665, and his *Diary* contains frequent references to the yard. Often he would be rowed across the Thames by watermen to Redriff (our Rotherhithe) and then walk through the fields to inspect the work before strolling back. Pepys stored some of his possessions at the Victualling Offices during the Great Fire, whilst his *Diary* also records that he sometimes brought his girlfriends to out of the way Deptford for an evening's uninterrupted pleasure. In the eighteenth century the ships *Resolution* and *Discovery* were fitted out here before accompanying Captain Cook on his last voyage. Today the Pepys Estate, opened in the 1960s by Lord Mountbatten, stands near the old site of the Victualling Warehouses and their entrance gates can still be seen on the east side of Grove Street.

Another famous diarist who knew this area well was John Evelyn who lived in Deptford for more than 40 years: hence our Evelyn Street. He moved into Sayes Court in 1653, attracted by its substantial house, orchard, garden and 100 acres of land, some of it at the bottom of this section of Rocque's map. Evelyn was a keen and expert gardener, often visited by his friend Samuel Pepys who noted 'among other rarities' in May 1665 'a hive of bees, so as being hived in glass, you may see the bees making their honey and combs mighty pleasantly.' Other sightseers who come to admire Evelyn's garden in the 1660s included Charles II and the Queen Mother.

Early in 1698 Czar Peter the Great hired Sayes Court when he journeyed to London in order to see the Deptford shipbuilding yards at work. He and his entourage departed after three months, leaving Evelyn to write sadly in his diary entry for 9th June 1698:

I went to Deptford to view how miserably the Tzar of Muscovy had left my house after three months making it his Court, having gotten Sir Christopher Wren his Majesty's surveyor and Mr. Loudon his Gardener to go down and make an estimate of the repairs, for which they allowed 150 pounds in their Report to the Lords of the Treasury.

In his book *Sylva* Evelyn refers again to his 'ruined garden', which makes it all the more surprising that today there is a Czar Street lying just off the modern map. Sayes Court was pulled down in the 1720s but there is a modern and well-kept garden on part of the site. A final significant legacy of Evelyn's association with Deptford is that one day in January 1671 whilst out walking in the neighbourhood he came across the then completely unknown sculptor and carver Grinling Gibbons working in a little hamlet. For introducing Gibbons to the court and securing him patronage, we owe Evelyn a debt for the magnificent Gibbons carvings which adorn several London churches.

Another important literary episode was placed here, by Jonathan Swift in his *Gulliver's Travels* of 1726. At the beginning of the book the publisher Richard Sympson explains that although Lemuel Gulliver lived in Redriff between voyages, 'growing weary of the concourse of curious people coming to him at his house in Redriff', he moved to Nottinghamshire but not before leaving certain papers in Sympson's hands: hence the book. Our modern map reveals a Gulliver Street just to the south of Redriff Road – Rocque's Rogues Lane.

The name of Deptford comes from the deep ford which had once existed beside the small river of Ravensbourne, and until the eighteenth century it remained a small village clustered around the church of St. Nicholas, the patron saint of sailors, parts of which still date back to the fourteenth century. The expansion of Deptford was confirmed by the building of St. Paul's Deptford by Thomas Archer in 1730, one of the 50 New Churches. Both St. Nicholas and St. Paul's survive to this day and are just off the bottom of Rocque's map. In the nineteenth century the opening of the Surrey Commercial Docks devoured the fields and countryside surveyed by Rocque in the 1740s. With the closure of these docks new uses are having to be found for the area.

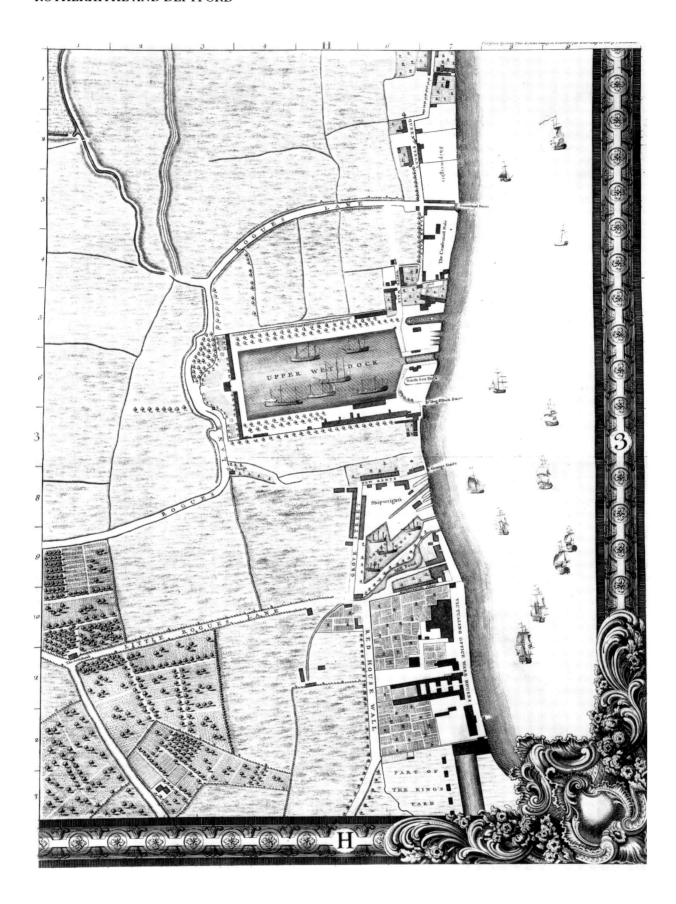

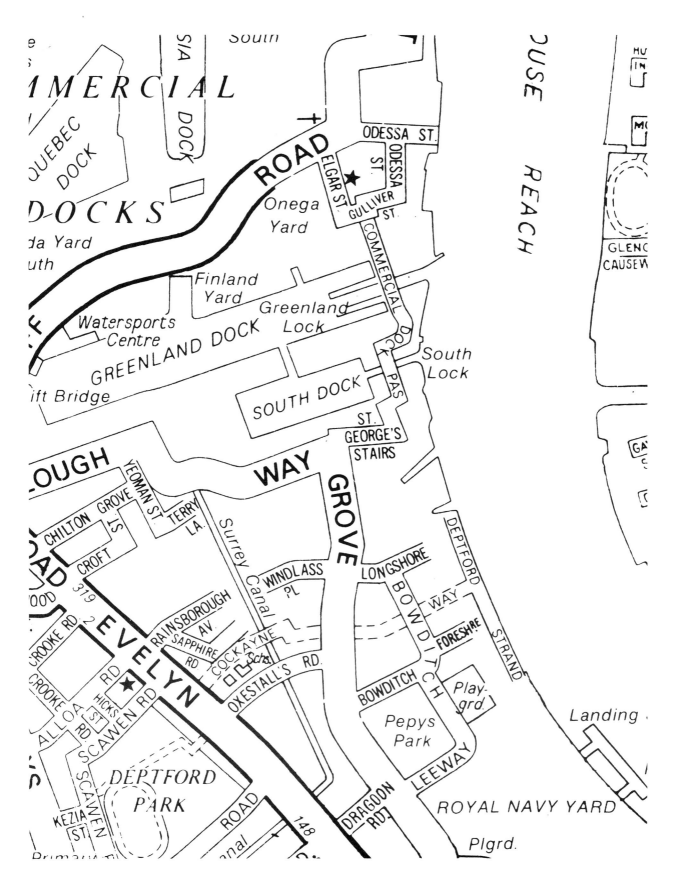

Notes

[1]Ann Callender (ed) *Godly Mayfair* (1980) p.2.

[2]Hugh and Pauline Massingham (eds) *The London Anthology* (1950) p.328.

[3]Simon Jenkins *Landlords to London* (1975) pp. 48-49.

[4]Sir John Summerson *Georgian London* (1978 ed.) p.111.

[5]David Piper *Companion Guide to London* (1977 ed.) p.72.

[6]Christopher Hibbert *The Personal History of Samuel Johnson* (1971) p.44.

[7]Dorothy George *London Life in the Eighteenth Century* (1966 ed.) p.54.

[8]Roy Porter *English Society in the Eighteenth Century* (1982) p.147.

[9]William Addison *English Spas* (1951) p.42.

[10]Mary Boast *The Story of Rotherhithe* (1980) p.9.

[11]Sheila Fairfield *The Streets of London* (1983) p.128.

[12]Simon Jenkins *Landlords to London* (1975) p.93.

[13]Denis Keeling 'The City of London and Tower Hamlets Cemetery' in *East London Papers* vol. 12 no.2, Winter 1969-70, p.126.

Suggested Further Reading

Useful for references and quotations are two sets of works published in the late nineteenth century: Thornbury and Walford's *Old and New London* (6 volumes) and Wheatley and Cunningham's *London Past and Present* (3 volumes). Neither are easily obtainable, unlike the indispensable *The London Encyclopaedia* (1983) edited by Ben Weinreb and Christopher Hibbert. Also useful are the relevant volumes in the continuing *Survey of London*.

There are countless local history publications produced by libraries, churches and community groups. The following is a short list of some of the best: Nick Bailey *Fitzrovia* (1981); Mary Boast *The Story of Rotherhithe* (1980), Mary Boast *The Story of the Borough* (1982), Mary Boast *The Story of Bermondsey* (1984 ed.); Colm Kerrigan *A History of Tower Hamlets* (1982); James Dowsing *Byways of Westminster* (no date), James Dowsing *Guide to Pimlico* (no date); John Oldland *A History of . . . St. Matthew* (1984); *St. Leonard's, Shoreditch* (1975); Mervyn Wilson *A Brief History of . . . St. Mary Magdalen* (1976).

However, the best way to get to know an area is simply to keep exploring it on foot.